Immigrant Youth Who Excel

Globalization's Uncelebrated Heroes

A volume in
International Perspectives on
Educational Policy, Research, and Practice

Series Editor:
Kathryn M. Borman, *University of South Florida*

International Perspectives on Educational Policy, Research, and Practice

Kathryn M. Borman, Series Editor

Immigrant Youth Who Excel: Globalization's Uncelebrated Heroes (2008)
by Rivka A Eisikovitis

The Challenges of Education in Central Asia (2006)
edited by Stephen P. Heyneman and Alan J. De Young

Surviving the Transition?
Case Studies of Schools and Schooling in the Kyrgyz Re (2006)
edited by Alan J. De Young, Madeleine Reeves, and Galina K. Valyayeva

Nordic Childhoods and Early Education: Philosophy, Research, Policy and Practice in Denmark, Finland, Iceland, Norway, and Sweden (2006)
edited by Johanna Einarsdottir and John A. Wagner

Educational Restructuring:
International Perspectives on Traveling Policies (2006)
edited by Sverker Lindblad and Tom Popkewitz

Immigrant Youth Who Excel

Globalization's Uncelebrated Heroes

by

Rivka A. Eisikovits
University of Haifa

Information Age Publishing, Inc.
Charlotte, North Carolina • www.infoagepub.com

Library of Congress Cataloging-in-Publication Data

Eisikovitis, Rivka A.
  Immigrant youth who excel : globalization's uncelebrated heroes / by Rivka A. Eisikovitis.
    p. cm. -- (International perspectives on educational policy, research, and practice)
  Includes bibliographical references.
  ISBN 978-1-59311-971-3 (pbk.) -- ISBN 978-1-59311-972-0 (hardcover) 1. Teenage immigrants--Education (Secondary)--Israel. 2. Teenage immigrants--Israel--Social conditions. I. Title.
  LC3747.I75E57 2008
  371.826'912--dc22

                                                                              2008027247

Printed in the United States of America

To my partner Zvi, eternally young immigrant who excels, and immigrant youths everywhere

Learning From the Experience of
Young Russian Immigrants in Israel

CONTENTS

ACKNOWLEDGMENTS

First and foremost I wish to express my deepest gratitude to the young immigrants who during the years of my study shared with me their stories, views and opinions so freely and so fully that it enabled me to retell them with accuracy and conviction.

I am grateful to Kathy Borman, series editor, for the invitation to publsih my book in this series and for her professional advice; to George F. Johnson, President, Information Age Publishing, for excellent collaborative work throughout the publishing process; to Rachel Lazarowitz, for her long lasting interest in my work; to Laura Sigad, my doctoral student and research assistant, for the valuable help she provided and to Genoveba Breitstein, for more than secretarial services. Recognition is also due to the University of Haifa for a year of sabbatical leave which I was able to devote to the completion of this book.

Thanks to my family in Boston: Nir, Masha, Sasha and Nina, for the warmth during the year spent together while I was working on this book. Finally, to my life-long partner and friend, Zvi, whose encouragement and belief in me were my driving force.

INTRODUCTION

Learning from immigrant students will sound to many like a nonsensical phrase. Why should one learn from them? Treated as a problem population by teacher adage (Kilman, 2005; Rosenbloom & Way, 2004; Tatar & Horenczyk, 2003), they should be dissolved, absorbed, assimilated—in other words—made to disappear, rather than becoming the subject of special attention. It is the contention of this book that we have a lot to learn from them. By "we," I refer to the educational community in receiving societies as well as to local peers. And high achieving immigrant students or, in short, "immigrants who excel" are our best potential teachers. They are the heroes of this volume and I will attempt to convince you, by following them through various stations on their way into their new society, of the valuable lessons they have in store for us.

Immigrant students the world over constitute more than 20% of the general student body. Some cannot, while others will not, blend in. However, research is primarily concerned with their educational achievements, comparing the academic performance of one group with that of another, and then with that of local students (Portes, 1995; Portes & Rumbaut, 2006; Zhou, 1997; Zhou & Xiong, 2005); attributing differential achievements to varying abilities to transcend school barriers (Bhatia & Ram, 2001; Fine, Pedraza, Futch, & Stoudt, 2007; Sloan, 2007). Less in the spotlight is the process of cross-cultural transition (Suárez-Orozco & Todorova, 2003). Yet, achievement and existential experience are indivisible, particularly for first generation youngsters who are also referred to as the "one-and-a-half generation," that is, young immigrants who have arrived in receiving societies prior to reaching adulthood (Rumbaut, 1991). I will argue that most of the lessons to be learned from them originate from the immigrant experience.

The large volume of immigrant students, constantly on the rise, is a direct by-product of intensifying globalization. This vast movement encompasses new types of young people. The taken-for-granted assumption of educational systems in host societies that immigrant students will readily assimilate is no longer valid. Many of them are ethnically retentive transnationalists (Remennick, 2007), children of diaspora migrant families (Bloch, Kennedy, Lightfoot, & Weynberg, 2006), who continue to regard their homeland as their cultural epicenter. Simply put, the tables have turned and the time has come for educational systems and their staffs to adjust to this new reality. The clamoring voices confronting schools for disregarding globalization as a fact of life, and failing to prepare the young for effective participation in it, are becoming louder and louder.

In two edited volumes devoted to the interface between globalization and precollegiate education, the first by Marcello Suárez-Orozco and Desirée Baolian Qin-Hilliard (2004), and the second by Suárez-Orozco (2007), editors and contributors highlight the qualities and competencies they deem requisite for young people's successful future involvement in this complex socioeconomic world order. Conspicuous among them is that present-day youth will grow up to live in a cross-national reality in the diverse spheres of their existence. Readiness for the challenges—risks along with opportunities—of such a lifestyle presupposes "cognitive skills, interpersonal sensibilities and cultural sophistication" (Suárez-Orozco & Qin-Hilliard, 2004, p. 2), as well as the ability to negotiate differences in order to collaborate with individuals of varying cultural and linguistic backgrounds in an atmosphere of tolerance and acceptance (p. 4).

It is my claim that compared to local youths in host societies, high achieving immigrant students are in a much better position to fulfill these conditions.[1] They are multilingual; have a built-in comparative perspective; as a result, are more reflective and critical, naturally develop the ability for situational use of identity, mostly adhere to their ethnic identity which is de-territorialized, and in general, have acquired skills to handle change. These characteristics render them less context-bound and more mobility prone. While local youth are likely to be monolingual and nonreflective concerning their sense of place, taking the latter, along with their national identity, for granted and, as such, are more territorially or locally bound. Hence, maximization of opportunities for fruitful encounters between members of the two groups,[2] in formal and informal educational contexts, promises mutual rapprochement, enhancing global fitness for both.

I chose to bring here the story of one such group that illustrates, rather compellingly, the experience of young immigrants who excel—youth from the European republics of the Former Soviet Union (FSU) who immigrated to Israel with their families during the 1990s. Let us see why they are such an outstanding case to analyze. Why do their chances to form mutual relationships with local peers theoretically exceed that of high achieving immigrant youngsters elsewhere? I say "theoretically exceed" because what indeed happens needs to be analyzed, a task I undertake in this volume. And last but not least, why is Israel an ideal context to potentially enable such a best case scenario to take place?

These Russian immigrants constitute one-fifth of the total Jewish population. With a relatively small cultural distance from the mainstream of the receiving society, their odds to meet the locals on an equal footing are optimal. High achievers, assertive, and confident in the cultural capital they bring along (Remennick, 2002), nowhere did an immigrant population make a bigger splash in the educational system of a host society.

Immigrant youths in large metropolitan centers in the United States or Canada, such as Los Angeles or Toronto, also constitute a sizeable portion of the student body, but their impact is more limited, due to heterogeneity in countries of origin and variability in achievement levels. Concerning Israel's position as an "ideal context"—its dedication to the absorption of Jewish immigrants, known as the "ingathering of exiles" from all over the globe (Bardach, 2005; Della Pergola, 2004; Sikron & Leshem, 1998) as part of its effort at nation building, make commitment to immigrant education a focal value. Again, the gap between the professed and the actual, needs to be studied. For all these reasons, learning about—and from—the Israeli experience promises to be an interesting and, I hope, rewarding endeavor.

Throughout the chapters, I will systematically compare the story of this group with that of other high achieving immigrant youths in the United States, Canada, and Europe, as well as Israel. I will make frequent reference to two ethnographies: *Accommodation Without Assimilation: Sikh Immigrants in an American High School* by Margaret Gibson (1988) and *Central American Refugees and U.S. High Schools* by Marcelo Suárez-Orozco (1989), due to the fact that these authors also consider the educational experiences of their subjects in their broad sociocultural contexts and examine the interactive effects of these facets. Although the above studies predate the era of globalization, their findings are highly relevant here because they highlight the perennial strengths of high achieving immigrant students of diverse backgrounds, a timeless resource whose ipso facto investigation is long overdue.

The other group of high achievers from the Israeli context, to whom I will relate, but from a different period, are the Transylvanians[3] who immigrated as adolescents in the early 1960s. In the conformist ethos of the newly born state, hardly over a decade from gaining its independence (in

1948), distinct otherness as a mode of educational or social participation for immigrant youngsters was inconceivable. Their narrative, which is also my personal one, delves into the long-lasting effects of expected cultural self-effacement as a price for social acceptance. This is the tale behind the tale of my life-long interest in the plight of young immigrants and personal commitment to making their transition smoother, that is, less painful. Showcasing the assertiveness of these Russian immigrant youths' style of cross-cultural adaptation and analyzing its root causes and effects should provide some catharsis to those of us who were offered nothing but the self-effacing route.

These comparisons through time and space bring out the unique along with the generalizable in the broad varying chronicles of immigrant youths. By sensitizing us to intergroup as well as within-group variation, they ward off the hazards of stereotypic thinking. Both these functions serve to promote an anthropology of youth migration.

A decade and a half of field research I had conducted on the adaptation styles of young immigrants from FSU in Israel from the 1990s on, yielded a long sequence of ethnographic and phenomenological studies, part of which serve as the basis for this book (Eisikovits, 1995a, 1995b, 2000, 2005, 2006, 2008; Eisikovits & Beck, 1990), extended and reanalyzed for its purposes. All studies were carried out in the northern part of the country, which absorbed the bulk of this immigration. They concentrated on youths originating from the urban centers of the European republics, the majority offspring of professional parents who were committed to the value of education. It was my belief that this background would contribute to a relatively unimpeded academic transition, rendering many of them success stories to be contemplated and emulated.

The book has two parts. Through a series of four interconnected studies, the first focuses on the youths' perceptions. We, meaning the reader and I, accompany them on their way into the new school, in chapter 1, and listen to evaluations of their academic and social experiences. In chapter 2, we learn about their informal social adaptation in various life settings, emphasizing gender differences in coping mechanisms. From here we proceed to public opinion formation in the course of preparation for first-time voting in a new political culture (chapter 3). Perceptions of the military, in chapter 4, as the last stage of compulsory postsecondary civic engagement for Israeli youngsters, close this section.

The second part places in the limelight the reactions of the educational system to catering to the needs of these immigrants who excel. Chapter 5 dwells on teachers' perspectives on the challenge they present, exploring differences in these perspectives according to their years of experience and subject matter area. Chapter 6 examines the organizational modus operandi of several schools, eliciting field-based models for handling immigrant students. Evolving from the latter, chapter 7 offers an anthropological approach for training teachers to work optimally with immigrant and culturally diverse students.

The programmatic epilogue offers an operational model for materializing the potential to enhance global participation for immigrants as well as locals, ensuing from the intercultural encounter.

Research procedures that are common to a number of studies are explained upon first mention. To aid in the visualization of adaptive patterns emerging from this large body of data—on both immigrant youth and educators in the receiving society—tables summarizing findings are provided for all but chapter 7. In addition to the comparative component, each chapter also includes an assessment of globalization proneness in light of its specific topic.

NOTES

1. See also Carola Suárez-Orozco (2004, p. 93) on the advantages of immigrants regarding globally adaptive competencies.
2. For the purpose of this discussion, I lump together all locals and all immigrants, respectively, referring to them as members of two distinct groups.
3. Transylvania is a large geographical region in the northwest of Romania, historically and culturally part of Hungary, and, at present, politically part of Romania.

PART I

YOUTHS SPEAK

CHAPTER 1

"MY EXPECTATIONS FROM SCHOOL?... HERE'S A LIST!"

The High School Compared and Assessed

The title itself denotes the uniqueness of the situation. Sergey,[1] the immigrant youngster quoted, feels comfortable to assume an assertive position, when provided a position of agency, and explain how the school could or, even should, best serve the group of immigrant students he is part of. The situation is so unusual because the common way in which the relationship between schools and immigrant students is conceptualized follows a very different route. The question normally posed by researchers is how to assist immigrant students overcome various school hurdles that bar their way in. The metaphor is clear: the school places the "barriers" and the immigrant student's job is to learn how to "jump" in order to cross them. The above quote reverses this axiomatic status, placing the immigrant students with their inherent needs in a central position, querying how the school could adapt to them.

The mass migration that followed the crumbling of the Eastern Bloc in the early 1990s created challenges of unprecedented magnitude for receiving societies. Educational systems were among the first to be mobilized for the effort of accommodating whole populations of immigrant children and youth, without much forewarning. Like in Israel, schools in

Immigrant Youth Who Excel: Globalization's Uncelebrated Heroes, pp. 9–34

other host societies, are on the frontline faced with the job of handling immigrant students, equipped with little professional knowledge and usually limited economic resources (Abedi, 2004; Portes & Rumbaut, 2006; Rumbaut, 1995).

One of the groups with the most urgent demands is the 16- to 18-year-old age bracket, students in the last 2 years of senior high school education. However, this is probably one of the least studied age groups in spite of the fact that age at immigration is recognized to be a crucial factor determining academic success (Cahan, Davis, & Staub, 2001; Eldering, 1997; Gibson, 1997; Rumbaut, 2004; Van Zanten, 1997). Urgent demands—since they have to pass matriculation or other forms of high-school leaving and college entrance exams, performance on which is likely to determine their professional future, opening or closing doors for them. The bulk of the literature on the socioeducational and emotional adjustment of youthful immigrant populations focuses on children and early adolescents (Aronowitz, 1984, 1992; Korpella, 2002; Pang, 2006; Zhou & Xiong, 2005; Waldinger & Feliciano, 2004). Seminal reviews on adolescent research (Brown, Larson, & Saraswathi, 2002; Butler & Gasson, 2005; Clark & Uzzell, 2002, 2006; Giordano, 2003) do not have entries on immigrant youth or late adolescents. Thus this age group with acute educational needs remains largely uncovered by both literatures. In this chapter I address this lacuna by examining how a group of immigrant youths from the Former Soviet Union (FSU) view their educational experience in the Israeli school system.

Following this massive wave of immigration I conducted an extensive intervention project in the Upper Hilltown school system to develop an anthropological action model for training teachers to work effectively with new immigrant and culturally diverse students (see chapter 7). This community has absorbed the highest percentage of Russian immigrants in Israel in the last decade. Of the high school student population, which numbered about 1,200 youngsters, 30%, was made up of new immigrant students (NIS) at the time of the intervention. "They are like a school within a school," said the head of the Department for New Immigrant Education. The high allocation of resources to NIS needs, resulting in an impressive variety of programs, reflects this community's commitment to immigrant absorption.

One of the recurrent self-critical statements voiced by high school teachers who participated in this community wide program was: "We are missing the boat with the older kids. Stressing academic performance under the pressure of the *Bagrut* [the matriculation exams][2] we neglect their social integration—an equally important part of our mission." Teachers consider social integration a primary goal in other societies, as well, since they are trained to be the "acculturative arm" of most immigrant receiving societies

(Suárez-Orozco & Suárez-Orozco, 2001; Taylor & Sobel, 2001; Zhou, 2003). Schools are mandated to be central vehicles of the nation state. In fact, the study shows what a favorable effect this "omission" had on these students' academic success. This is a common finding. Gibson (1988; 1995), Suárez-Orozco (1989) and Suárez Orozco and Suárez-Orozco (1995) also describe how positively their successful immigrant students they describe, Punjabis and Central Americans in the United States, respectively, reacted to the school's nonintervention to alter their ethnic or cultural beliefs and believed this enhanced their academic achievement.

THE STUDY

Initial interviews with these students and participant observation in their various school interaction contexts were conducted during the year of migration as part of my work on the development of the previously mentioned anthropological action research model. However, at that time it was too early to attempt a meaningful study of the students' perspectives on their education in the new social environment. My field work experience taught me that studying first generation immigrant youngsters who had spent less than three years in the new country produces meager results. During this time they are undergoing the acute stage of their cross-cultural transition (Anderson, 1994). Most of them had neither the language ability to express themselves fluently in Hebrew, nor the reflective distance necessary for a comparative assessment of experiences in the two systems. Consequently, I decided to return 2 years later for a second round of in-depth interviews with some 20 of these youths, 10 males and 10 females, who were now in their senior year.

To gain a broad perspective, informants of both sexes participating in a variety of programs available to new immigrant youths in this school were interviewed (Denzin & Lincoln, 1994; Fontana & Frey, 1994, p. 365). Topics discussed included reasons for immigration, satisfaction with the new school as compared to schooling experiences in the country of origin, future career goals and how immigration has affected them, relations with host national and same culture peers, and such broader issues as the formation of a national identity. These topics required the youth to adopt a comparative approach to their educational experiences in the two countries, what Suárez-Orozco (1989) refers to as a "dual frame of reference." Such an approach provides educators in the new society primary source information on the educational milieu these students came from and the study skills they brought along—both necessary for designing effective programs for them. The level of detail immigrant youth will be willing to go into in sharing their recollections, hinges upon their evaluation of the quality of education received in their country of origin. Informants who consider the quality of their prior schooling to be equal or higher than their present one, as is the case with these youngsters and the Transylvanians, will be naturally more motivated to describe these memories at length (Eisikovits, 1995).

Although the NIS were a diverse group of young people, the content analysis of the interviews from both rounds and the participant observation data revealed three distinctive profiles whose members' encounters with host country peers, school experiences, and attitudes toward the wider social sphere differed considerably (Holstein & Gubrium, 1994, pp. 267–268).

Profile I was comprised of informants who came with definite future career plans and whose choices were largely unaffected by immigration, the *determined-unaffected.* This group mainly consisted of high-ability young males with talents in mathematics and the sciences.

Profile II was made up of talented young people with clear career plans in the arts and the humanities. Members of this group, which was predominantly female in composition, found their career choices intensely affected by immigration, the *determined-affected.*

Profile III included average ability motivated youngsters of both sexes who arrived without definite plans, the *undecided,* and were thus highly susceptible to immigration induced educational changes.

Profile I and II informants tended to be more sophisticated and articulate on a variety of issues. Conversely, Profile III informants were found to be less verbal and lacking in crystallized attitudes on topics discussed in the interviews. The three profiles turned out to be approximately equal in size. Contrary to my expectation the *undecided* was not the largest group. This should be understood in light of the highly pragmatic orientation of the former Soviet educational system that urged youngsters of mediocre abilities, along with those of outstanding talents, to formulate career goals at a relatively early age and channel their efforts in that direction (Markowitz, 2000; Remennick, 2007). In the USSR., generalist education was traditionally identified with "bourgeois decadence" and viewed as wasteful (Pearson, 1990). It should be noted that my interest was not in the relative size of the profiles, which might have been random, but rather in exploring how the members of each one experienced their socioacademic integration (LeCompte & Preissle, 1993). Looking for profiles in this closely knit group of youngsters, characterized by high conformity to cultural rules, provided safeguards against stereotype formation. The emergence of these subgroups allowed a more thorough search for the operative principles of smaller units of analysis. For example, having found that the study group was divisible according to career orientation gave me further insight into within-group diversity, helping to disclose additional motifs in the informants' lifeway. Throughout the study I continued to test the viability of the profiles as guiding analytic tools.

Analysis of the interviews indicated that although on some topics the informants' attitudes were associated with their respective profiles, on other matters the views they expressed were not connected to their profiles but were common to the whole group. In the latter case, the attitudes are referred to as "general." Because the profiles are heuristic constructs derived inductively from the content analysis of the interviews and thus are related to the emergent themes, the findings are first presented and discussed thematically, across the profiles. Subsequently a table that graphically presents general as well as profile-linked positions is provided. Finally, the distinguishing features of each profile's adaptive route are examined in the concluding section.

IMMIGRATION: WHY AND HOW

This section encompasses reasons for immigration as perceived by the informants, the part the informants played in the decision-making process that preceded the immigration and the effect of their pre-immigration preparation on their ability to cope with the new social context and on general attitudes toward the receiving society.

The main reason for immigration, or more precisely, the reason the parents presented to the informants, was to ensure a better future for these youths. The educational opportunities of many seemed in jeopardy because of rising anti-Semitism and the overall state of chaos in the FSU. Although the rationale for immigration was directly related to them, most of the interviewees had not participated in this decision. This motif—the future of the children as a rationale for migration along with the totally passive role allotted to the youngsters (regardless of age) in the decision making—seems to be universal and appears frequently in studies of immigration (Suárez-Orozco, 2004; Zhou, 1997; Zhou & Xiong, 2005).

In the present study this was a general pattern. None of the informants had any input in this process, which they defined as "grown-up business." Most of these adolescents accepted unquestioningly the appropriateness of their parents' action on their behalf on a matter of lifelong consequence. Immigrant children and youths' reactions also seem to be universal (Markowitz, 1996; Pang, 2006; Remennick, 2007). But in chapter 2 we will also hear a few discordant voices, complaining about friends and social networks left behind. However, at this stage the informants were operating out of a different set of assumptions on parent-child or rather parent-youth relations from what is considered normative in most Western family systems (Bronfenbrenner, 1970, Tomiak, 1986; Remennick, 2007). They viewed their families primarily as coping units facing an oppressive society. In accordance with this perception, individual family members subordinated personal desires to the common goal of "beating the system" (Horowitz, 1989). Some informants were puzzled by my question on whether they had been "consulted" or "included in the decision making" on immigration. Nina could not see what I meant by "being consulted." "Why should they consult me? My parents know what is best for me." This tone of docility represents the majority pattern in this sequence of studies. The young people are respectful of their parents, aware of their hardships and sacrifices. These sentiments are also common to children of immigration in other contexts (see Suárez-Orozco, 1989, for similar findings).

Furthermore, they did not think the term "decision making" reflected what had occurred. In their perception, their immigration had not been motivated by free choice. As Boris put it: "Rumors were that the situation in Russia[3] will get worse. So, we ran, we didn't 'decide,' " I stood corrected. Boris' statement suggests a refugee style migration (Gibson, 1997; Ogbu & Simons, 1998). Making host society members understand their predicament to prevent stereotyping based on misconceptions, on this or any other matter, was considered a top priority by the informants. The situation of the interview conducted by an adult who is an academic and an interviewee who is a young immigrant is, by definition, power differentiated. Nevertheless, most informants insisted on correcting my use of concepts and felt free to do so. This assertiveness is unique to members of this study group. I did not come across similar behavior patterns in interviewing my own age mates—compatriots from Transylvania. Nor did I learn about such manifestations from other studies of young immigrants. I will return to this feature in continuation.

The importance of educating the young generation notwithstanding, many families were pressured to leave the USSR due to a rampant mass hysteria that compelled all those who could leave to do so. Anti-Semitism, I was told, was often spurred by envy toward those Jews who were fortunate enough to be granted exit visas. In other words, more push than pull factors were operative. However, Israel was not a primary destination on either religious or ideological grounds. In fact, many would have preferred the United States and settled for Israel when the United States no longer granted refugee status to Russian Jews. Emigration was the only way to secure a safer and financially better future. In contradiction with Boris' assessment, Remennick (2007) sums up the circumstances of this migration wave as follows: "The emigration decisions of Russian Jews in the 1990s were driven by pragmatic rather than ideological considerations; that is, the careful weighing of the push and pull factors (or gains vs. losses) in the FSU vis-à-vis possible destinations abroad" (p. 43).

Although my informants should be viewed as passive protagonists in their families' migration, they have been surrounded by this survivalist atmosphere and have internalized the value base underlying this mentality. Several expressed it as an opportunistic attitude toward their host society and newly adopted country. For example, Arkady, an articulate exponent of the *determined-unaffected* profile, treated having arrived in Israel pragmatically. No emotions seemed involved. He had no preference between Israel and the United States, and said, "I don't know how things would have worked out in the U.S. It's all a question of luck. One has to make the best of what one has. People can live everywhere." Then as an afterthought he added nostalgically, "I loved Kiev very much." The unspoken association of ideas was unequivocal. Kiev stood for all the familiar places Arkady had left behind and he no longer expected to feel emotional attachment to new places. Therefore, where he lived became a matter of convenience. There was sadness in his voice, a reverberation of loss, not only of place but also of his youth. An attitude of opportunistic pragmatism, such as exemplified by Arkadi, was more characteristic of Profile I informants, who had high hopes for personal success and were relatively less context-sensitive, than it was of Profile II and III informants.

Although the informants were not consulted in the decision-making process, some were better prepared for immigration than others. That seemed to have made a considerable difference in their ability to adapt to the new reality awaiting them in their country of destination. For example, members of the Transylvanian study group reported thorough preparation for emigration conducted by the parents in the long years spent awaiting their exit visas. Education of the young became the major emigration related activity since the realities of life in the totalitarian regime of Communist Romania during the 1950s precluded any other form of preparation. Investment in the education of children gave a sense of limited control over the future (Eisikovits, 1995c). The parents' meticulous planning for the future through their children's education was directed at both school and extracurricular activities. Mathematics and the sciences, seen as largely language-transcending disciplines, were cultivated in preparation for immigration. Out-of-school activities were paid for privately and included the study of Western languages and instrumental music. The choice of instrument was often influenced by considerations of mobility, with a preference for portable instruments such as the violin or accordion. Playing an instrument well was seen as part of a well-rounded education and as a skill that would offset the effects of the anticipated temporary decrease in verbal ability In sum, the plan was to equip the children with cross-culturally applicable skills and a capacity for self-sufficiency in as many domains as possible.

In the present case, preparation could mean a range of actions, from sending youngsters to orientation courses on Israel offered by the Jewish Agency in various urban centers throughout the FSU, to just holding family discussions on setting realistic expectations. Unprepared informants of both genders experienced the transition as most traumatic. Sergey explained: "I didn't know I was a Jew for a long time. I was shocked. Going to Israel was like a dream. I thought it would never really happen." For many the possibility of breaking out from that closed world seemed unreal and acquired a mythical quality. Conversely, those who had some preparation appeared more at ease coping with new challenges and entertained a generally favorable orientation toward the new country and the people. This again, was a general finding. It should be noted that pre-emigration preparation of the young is not treated in the literature. As earlier noted, in most immigration research the topic is summed up by statements to the effect that children and youth are passive participants in the process.

Getting back to this study, I found that once in Israel, the parents acted in accordance with their declared commitment to the education of their children. The interviewees reported that even those parents who were unemployed managed to mobilize their resources to purchase computers or hire private tutors for English, Hebrew, or math to help their children gain entry into the most competitive high school programs, or to boost their grade point averages on the *Bagrut*.

While the Transylvanians filled their pre-immigration years with the educational preparation of their young, the Russians, whose exodus was hastier, paid their tribute in the new country. Either way, both groups expressed through their pre- or post-immigration activities the high value East-European Jews attributed to education.

SCHOOLING: HERE AND THERE

In this section the informants' approach to their past school experiences is discussed and their expectations from their new school are spelled out. These expectations and relationships with teachers are assessed comparatively. Relevant background information on educational policy, school structure, and curricular issues for the two systems is included to help provide a context for the opinions expressed by the informants.

When asked about school atmosphere in their country of origin, the interviewees declined to make generalizations, claiming "Every school, every classroom is different. Here people like to talk about all Russian schools as tough." Multilevel resistance to generalization comes across. They oppose stereotyping tendencies of the locals concerning things Russian, equally refusing to use generalizations when asked to relate to their own experiences. Their reticence can be explained in several ways. First, as products of a totalitarian system, they had a tradition of mistrust toward authority figures. This attitude was transferred to interactions with Israeli officials, as well (Horowitz, 1989; Remennick, 2007). Generalizing meant "knowing too much." Taking a stand on issues was considered dangerous in such a context. Therefore, individuals preferred to speak of personal experiences in descriptive terms. The interviewees' young age supported their claim of limited general knowledge to a great extent. So when asked about school atmosphere, many chose to concentrate on differences between such material details as size, upkeep of buildings, or organizational matters in the two systems. "Schools in Israel are much larger. There we learned in shifts, younger kids in the morning, older kids in the afternoon," Larissa said.

"Was it a beautiful building?" I tried to follow her lead and approach the topic from the physical angle.

"No, it was old, but they remodeled it. It was clean," she replied, steering back to safer ground.

"Was there a pleasant atmosphere?" I insisted.

"No, only in my class. [Finally!] I had a wonderful teacher, the same one since first grade. She taught us not to hate each other. In my brother's class they were fighting all the time."

"The class" was the broadest level of generalization they were willing to "risk" on this topic. It is interesting to compare the Transylvanian case on this point. Listening to these adult informants idealize their pre-emigration school experience—it was "like a small Eton," Nira said— (Eisikovits, 1995c, p. 176) it becomes crystal clear how vivid in their long term memory the insult of having been deprived of their cultural uniqueness as immigrant high school students more than 3 decades earlier, still was. Back to Larissa and the crucial information she provided in her last statement. It demonstrates the crucial role played by individual teachers in influencing the quality of education of their students, regardless of hostility in the larger system. The Transylvanian case brings out this theme even more forcefully. The informants talk emotionally about the role of Dora, the elementary school teacher, in their lives. For this group immigration to Israel was the second cross-cultural encounter. The first was the passage from their Hungarian speaking homes to the Romanian school. Dora, who was bilingual and bicultural herself, served as a culture broker facilitating her students' gradual transition to the new linguistic medium. She systematically introduced them to the second language without their experiencing the sense of deficiency or disadvantage which so often accompanies the minority child's induction into the dominant culture. Moreover, being of the parents' age group and personally acquainted with many of them, Dora was supportive of the high achievement expectations they had for their children. She was both equipped and willing to take an extra effort to smooth their passage into the regimented school climate while continuing to strengthen their motivation. She became a most meaningful figure in the lives of these families. This partnership between parents and teacher accounted for a considerable part of the children's educational success. Although strict and demanding, all interviewees concurred that she made them feel they really mattered to her. Many corresponded with her for years after leaving Tirgu-Mures.[4] "Her strength pulled me through the hardest times in the Israeli school," Omri said. "You had to prove yourself even when she was no longer there. There was a sense you couldn't let her down because she believed in us," he concluded (Eisikovits, 1955c, p. 195).

I dwelled on this point because it convincingly brings forth the importance of deconstructing the immigrant students' educational history in order to better understand their performance and behavior in the receiving country. Both examples bear witness to the fact that only through comparison can immigrant youths make meaning of their new school activities. In other words, comparison is the life blood of the immigrant experience. These youths build on the positive energy gained from past performance to define their place in the new context. Through this cognitive operation the past is transformed into an active part of current educational experience, incorporated in it. This reflective mechanism is at the base of immigrant youths' adaptability.

Returning to our profiles, we learn that many of the informants, mostly the *undecided*, idealized their former schooling as a time of perceived personal competence, as opposed to their bewilderment in the new school with rules and expectations they did not yet fully comprehend. One expression of this practice was the imposition of a time freeze while comparing their activities in the two educational systems. This epistemological fallacy, attributable to confusion or cognitive overload, manifested itself in a lack of differentiation between their ages and the level of the tasks they were required to perform at two distinct points in time. Some illustrative statements were: "There I learned for fun, here I learn for grades," or "We had fewer written exams there."[5]

On the whole, the position of the youngsters described in these two studies was clearly more advantageous than that of immigrant youths from the Punjab described by Gibson (1988) or the young Central American refugees portrayed by Suárez-Orozco (1989). Neither of the latter groups had the luxury of relying on a positive past image, for their own different reasons, whether their schools were less advanced (Gibson, 1988), or that they attempted to escape from a war-torn zone (Suárez-Orozco, 1989). They had no favorable past scenario to lean back on to counterpoise the "negative mirror image", which the locals, particularly their peers, presented them (Suárez-Orozco, 2004, p. 182).

Relating to the Russians, Samoff (1991) describes the role of schools in the post-Communist era (p. 17) as follows: "in transition societies, the reproductive character of schools has overwhelmed its role in establishing and nurturing democratic practices. The schools, the society, and the transition have all suffered." In this context I was interested to find out whether these youths had had any first hand experiences brought about by the state of flux that ensued from the crumbling of the former regime. In other words, the question was whether the chaos of transition had filtered down to the level of the schools, and if it had, what some of its expressions were. I received a few unspecific reports on "hooliganism" and beatings in the schools. "We were afraid to go, it wasn't safe." Also, absenteeism went unobserved and irregular attendance became a quasi-norm. "After my parents told me we were going to Israel, I stayed home with my sister," Olga said. "There was no point in going to school. We were leaving anyway and the teacher didn't mind." In certain cases such situations would last for months.

The transition period before leaving created a hiatus in the educational experience of these youths. The life course of the family, as a whole was disrupted. Irregular school attendance for an extended duration was a marker of this "time unusual." Suarez-Orozco (1989) also reports about a similar phenomenon among his informants due to the civil war. This made readjustment to fixed schedules, regular attendance, and the generally heavy work load awaiting these informants in the high-pressure senior high school in the host country particularly hard in both cases. For the Transylvanians who invested long-term multigenerational effort to educational preparation for immigration, disorientation reached its climax in the new context upon finding the schools so unprepared to receive them.

On arrival in Israel, all NIS spent a few months in an *Ulpan*, an intensive Hebrew language and cultural orientation program. Instruction here occurred in small groups and was largely individualized. Following this, depending on ability and inclination, those with a mathematics and science interest were placed in integrated classes along with veteran Israeli students. These disciplines are considered to be relatively less linguistically determined. However, youngsters with talents in the humanities and social studies, which are regarded as relatively more language dependent, studied in an NIS program specially designed to suit their level of proficiency in Hebrew. Because of the crucial importance of the matriculation exam, educators in their new school made every effort to promote these students' success and compensate for their language difficulties in several ways: by offering special exams and programs for NIS in basic Hebrew, oral testing with Russian speaking examiners, or bonuses for those who opted to take the regular exams.

Most Israeli academic senior high schools employ curricular tracking. The mathematics and science tracks are seen as more prestigious than the humanities and social studies tracks (Ichilov, 1991). Whereas both Profile I (*determined-unaffected*) and Profile II (*determined-affected*) informants recognized the advantages of the diversified curriculum, members of the undecided group regarded this variety as threatening. Because they experienced the present from a vantage point of academic disadvantage, they perceived curricular tracking that lowered the age at which career decisions were made, as increasing their handicap by excluding them from the prestigious options "before [they] even had a chance to try." Retrospectively reassessing the uniform curriculum in the Russian schools, these students found it more egalitarian by comparison. They used the comparison to complete the puzzle of their life course, filling in the missing parts.

Although they were skeptical about planned change and the systems level interventions intended to bring it about, members of Profile I and II had a well defined position on how they would like to "adjust" their new school to their own objectives. Dima spelled it out:

> There is no need for all this social stuff, afternoon activities, vacation activities. We had enough nagging like that in Russia. I don't want this interference in my personal life. Instead, school should provide good teachers, tutors, the best equipment to enable us to learn. Information on how to get accepted to the universities is also important.

Expectations were defined on the personal level. Vladimir, another Profile I interviewee, believed that "students, as individuals, pursue their own goals in school and get different things out of their experiences depending on their input and expectations." Their microlevel interest notwithstanding, these youths had a macrolevel comparative overview of the two school systems in terms of time budgeting, curricular emphases, preferred learning styles, and so forth. Tania's remarks were representative:

> Israeli schools squeeze you out completely during the last two years before the *Bagrut*. In Russia the effort was more stretched out. So it wasn't so hard. There they tested you on facts; here, mainly in literature, civics, and history; they want to make sure you understand different processes and can analyze them.

These assertive youngsters were willing to "teach" their new educators, who were unaccustomed to such consumer consciousness among their students, "what school should do for us." These were the words of Sergey, who described himself as "an egoist, not an optimist, and not a pessimist." He added: "You ask about my expectations from school? Here's a list!" This self-conscious, utilitarian statement makes him sound more precocious than he would have probably liked to perceive himself. The informants readily supplied the kind of information Entwisle (1990) called for, in her list of topics on adolescent-school relationships that need to be researched. Among other things, she called for more attention to be paid to the effect adolescents have on their schools to counterbalance the prevailing research emphasis on how schools affect adolescents (p. 221).

In the self-reliant, predominantly Profile I position described above, teachers constituted just one item on "the list." Attitudes toward teachers ranged, however, from this utilitarian stance to an admission that teachers played a cardinal role in their school experiences. The extent and quality of the NIS' interactions with teachers in their new school environment varied with their program or curricular track assignment. Profile III youths were evidently most susceptible to teacher attitudes. In the integrated classes they tended to feel lost, because they had no one to turn to for emergencies or when they needed professional guidance. In Alec's "integrated" class the instruction coordinator, a history teacher by specialization, met her students three times weekly, when the NIS in her class were scheduled to be in a special language program. Because she hardly ever saw them, she failed to remember their names. This made it normative for the nonimmigrant students not do so, either.

In the all NIS class, on the other hand, the students received more personal attention. Teachers tried their best to communicate with them. They had a highly committed coordinating teacher who made them feel free and relaxed. Dina explained: "She is like a friend. Here teachers are more open to discuss students' personal problems. In Russia the teachers' role was limited to teaching their subjects." Profile II informants were appreciative of the new organizational arrangement. According to Sveta,

> It was made especially for us. I really like it. I am not anonymous here. Where else would I have a special *Bagrut* exam written just for me in musicology. It would have never happened without Rachel's [the coordinating teacher] stubborn fight with the bureaucracy in Jerusalem.

Others praised all the career information, brochures, and guest lectures to which she exposed them. Sveta continued: "My closest friends are all from Russia anyway, and I have other opportunities to meet *Sabras*[6] outside of school."

But Profile Ill students in the above program were more concerned with the isolating effects of this class. Anna felt "it's like a ghetto." Here the double effect of "exclusion" from the more prestigious track and the high value placed on the integrative aspects of school interacted to create a sense of discontent.

LOOKING AHEAD: PLANNING A CAREER

The crystallization of career choices for Israeli youth is deferred into their early twenties due to their long compulsory military service. Most American young people also engage in definitive career planning at about the same age, at the end of their college years, because their undergraduate studies mostly provide a generalist education. So the phenomenon of 17- to 18-year-old Russian immigrant students with such meticulous future plans was a novelty to their Western educators (Horowitz, 1989; Lieblich, 1993). But long-range planning in education as in all other spheres of life was the essence of Communist morality.

Although the majority of Soviet high schools remained untracked by curriculum under Glasnost, Pearson (1990) maintains that specialized elitist high schools for mathematics and the sciences continued to function and attract primarily male students. Several of my male informants attended such schools and considered these areas of study "professions of the future everywhere in a technological world." They sounded well-informed about study options and employment opportunities in Israel, often incorporating military service into their plans as a desirable career avenue. The army offers interesting jobs and favorable work conditions in engineering and the sciences.

Pearson (1990) also notes that many more females than males chose the arts or humanities as their field of self-actualization. Those relatively few Profile II female informants who insisted on staying within their areas of strength in the arts or humanities encountered opportunities for self-actualization and found organizational support for their career planning in school. For example, Sveta, the musician mentioned earlier, felt that the encouragement she received in school energized her to pursue her artistic career, which she was about to give up.

However, Katia's case was more characteristic of the Profile II females' experiences in their new school. She had attended a selective school for languages back in the FSU, which prepared students for careers in journalism and simultaneous and literary translation. Her reaction to my question concerning her future plans in Israel conveyed utter confusion. "I don't know anymore because I switched completely" [to a science and mathematics major]. My first impression was that this had been a deliberate choice on her part. Further investigation revealed it to have been a negative choice prompted by well-intentioned teacher intervention to "Make life easier for her. As a math major she simply needs less Hebrew," one of the teachers explained. This pattern of being "switched out" of their area of preference mostly involved females in my sample. As a result, gifted students, like Katia, who had career plans as carefully designed as those of Profile I males, lost their edge and had to compete with "strong mathematicians," both veteran Israelis and NIS, almost all males (Deegan, 1993). Needless to say their self-confidence suffered in the process. This finding is supported by Burton's (1990) contention that in most societies success in mathematics is gender related.

Ichilov (1991), in her study of political socialization and schooling effects among Israeli adolescents, also found that the involvement, efficiency, and freedom of speech of males were reinforced through schooling to a greater extent than they were among females and that, generally speaking, schooling had a greater positive effect for males than for females. Taking this line of argumentation to an extreme, Riordan (1990) claims, on the basis of cross-national data, that mixed-sex schooling damages females' self-image by promoting males' education through tracking, unconscious bias in teaching methods, counseling practices, and so forth. Therefore, he concludes that single-sex schooling is the most advantageous educational alternative for females.

Feminist criticism of the negative effects of schooling on females was substantiated in the present case by the fact that many of these capable, future-oriented female students lost their sense of direction and found themselves closer to the holding positions characteristic of the *undecided* group on a variety of issues by the end of high school. Although Profile I and II youths of both sexes remained generally committed to the importance of higher education, Profile II females expressed more apprehension about the future. "I don't want to be an engineer, but since I am in a science class I don't know much about other options," was a common reaction. Some were doubtful whether planning for tertiary education was a realistic goal for them.

PEER WORLDS: DISTINCT AND SEPARATE

The low intensity intergroup relations that did not extend beyond the confines of the school were variously interpreted. Mikhail, a Profile I interviewee, made a sharp distinction between relationships with classmates and relationships with personal friends. "School is not a place for socializing. All my personal friends come from Russia. They have different values, and they like a different atmosphere." In Israeli society boundaries between the personal and the public sphere, and thus friend-ship networks, are less clear (Eisikovits & Karnieli, 1992; Weissbrod, 2002). But because the public sphere of life in Russia was an area of high social intervention, exercising free choice in defining one's circle of inti-mates became crucial. Mikhail's emphasis on the distinction between situ-ational and selected relationships was an assertion of his uniqueness and was set against the depersonalizing treatment of individuals in the con-text of mass migration.

To illustrate the differences in values between his friends and Israeli youths he made the following point:

> Let's take discipline, for example. I see it in a very positive way. It allows people to bring out the best in themselves in school, the army, at work. I need it to concentrate. The *Sabras* see school requirements for discipline as a restriction of their freedom. They don't realize that it would help them do better in school. School is for learning, it is not a place to be free.

He qualified his statement by adding, "I shouldn't say this. I don't really know enough people here." The implication was that he and his friends saw the *Sabras* as less sophisticated and as a result unable to distin-guish between situation-appropriate behavioral codes. But as if amazed by his own temerity he retracted to more solid ground: "Anyway, lack of discipline is self-defeating. All this noise gives everyone a headache."

Contrary to the mostly Profile I distinction between in-group and out-group relations, for Profile III informants the integrative social function of the school and relations with host country peers were important. They would have liked more social activities such as school parties and trips. These were seen as opportunities for more closeness between Israeli kids and NIS. Profile I interviewees disliked these field trips and found them too monotonous. Olga remarked:

> All we do is go for miles in the desert and look at stones, to follow in the footsteps of heroes from the past. But all the stones look the same. We should go to museums. When we were in Eilat [a popular Red Sea resort], we didn't even go to the beach. [We] need to do more fun things.

Their matter-of-fact attitude toward the new country prevented them from identifying with the *Sabras'* enthusiasm over those "stones" that told a story that some of them did not know and some may not have cared to find out.

Profile II and III youngsters tended to view themselves as "rejected" or "ignored" by their Israeli peers, whereas Profile I informants described these relations in more reciprocal terms such as "we have little contact." Accordingly, whereas Profile I informants would say, "we don't mind" and "we don't have to be friends to learn in the same class," Profile II and Ill informants were deeply hurt by the depersonalized attitude they encountered: "They call all the females Lena. To them we all look alike." Because they were already suffering from a loss of self-esteem due to the shift in their major, Profile II females in the integrated mathematics and science classes took it particularly hard.

On the other hand, several members of the *determined-unaffected* group admitted:

> We don't make efforts to get closer to them either. During breaks it's more comfortable to speak Russian with other new immigrant kids. So we don't push it too hard, on our part. Besides, they have their own problems. They also come from all different classes.

Whether this was a case of "rejecting the rejector" or a function of a higher degree of sophistication that allowed spokesmen of this profile to stress in-group affinity and downplay the hurt of rejection is hard to determine. The verbally conveyed message indicated the choice of an additive approach to social integration (Gibson, 1995, 2001; Hurh & Kim, 1984; Portes & Rumbaut, 2006) and concentration on academic success. These youths were also more self-conscious of the inhibiting effect of language barriers, which impede "real communication" with Israeli peers. Sergey explained:

> They have such a different mentality that it is hard to tell them a joke, for example. I need to explain so much, to work so hard for a joke. It's ridiculous. Then they don't get my humor and I feel so stupid. I won't even try again.

Amplification of intercultural variance was used to account for this state of affairs. "We have different interests, read different books, listen to different music. Israeli kids don't read. They don't talk about books like us." Such "us" versus "them" rhetoric ran throughout the interviews, interspersed with vehement exhortations against "block vision" or mutual stereotyping, such as: "People are all different. Like everyone has five fingers and each is different." This lack of awareness of the discrepancy between style and content is yet another reflection of their confusion.

Profile II and III students conceded they felt that immigrating during late adolescence, with the difficulties characteristic of that age and the additional challenge of the *Bagrut*, was "just too much." *Bagrut* literally means maturity in Hebrew. The added symbolic function of the exams as a rite of passage for these youngsters was evident.

Profile I interviewees who did not find the academic challenges in their new school too hard to handle tended to think that "this was great timing assuming one had a choice." The reason given was that they were old enough to remember their past and to critically assess what aspects of the new culture fit them. "Had I come earlier I would not have seen the differences. Had I come later it might have been too hard to change," Vladimir said. These informants experienced their cross-cultural transition and exposure to alternative lifestyles as a source of personal enrichment.

However, a common difficulty noted by all these NIS was a decline in the quality of communication with their parents, which resulted in a pervasive sense of loneliness. "They have enough problems of their own, how can I add to that," was a typical remark. Mirsky and Kaushinsky (1989) who studied the cross-cultural adaptation patterns of university students who immigrated without their families, highlight the crucial role of SCP in warding off serious pathology. This finding also seems to apply to this group of late adolescents who, although they immigrated with their families, could not depend on them for emotional support. Thus same culture peers became all important. This topic is treated extensively in the next chapter.

WHO IS AN ISRAELI

On the issue of national identity formation there was also a range of opinions. The more secure claimed: "All of us are Israelis, each in his or her way, not just the *Sabras*." Others, like Olga, Larissa, and Dina, felt that "as long as the *Sabra*s refuse to take us in we cannot become Israelis." They have internalized the ethnocentric message that acceptance by the mainstream is a precondition for the formation and manifestation of one's national identity. A middle position was represented by Sergey's view: "If I were asked about my nationality by foreigners abroad I would definitely identify myself as an Israeli. But inside Israel, I still can't. The *Sabra*s don't think I belong here," he said with a half smile.

Those who held the first position (mostly Profile I informants) admitted they should play an active role and become knowledgeable about social and political issues. "Otherwise we will never break out from this narrow circle." They were willing to assume a fair share of the blame for their voluntary self-isolation, adopting a layered perception of their sociocultural identity. Because school experiences and the formation of attitudes toward the larger society are related (see chapter 6 for a discussion of this topic), these positions largely coincided with profile affiliation, assertive for Profile I and mostly passive or reactive for the other two.

The army was believed to play a salutary role as a promoter of social integration. In addition to its career enhancing function, military service was universally considered a proper vehicle for providing more informal opportunities to mingle with *Sabras*, thereby boosting mutual intergroup relations. The informants viewed military service as a less pressured period in the future, and several expressed hopes to meet Israelis on a one-to-one basis in that new context. "We'll get to know them as people, they will get to know us." Again unaware of the style-content incongruity, the informants were still not ready to relinquish their "we" identity even hypothetically in such a future perspective. This tenacious cultural adhesion and strong identification with a group of intimates seemed to function as a replacement for their lost anchor in space, which Marris (1980) calls the experience of uprootedness. Views on the military service are discussed at length in chapter 4.

So far I have presented and discussed the findings of the study comparatively. Now I would like to proceed to a more graphic portrayal of the informants' positions according to their profile affiliation. It is to this end that Table 1.1 is offered.

CONCLUDING REMARKS

Much research on immigrant students deals with the socioeducational accommodation of children and youths from Third World countries in receiving societies that are technologically more advanced (Eldering & Kloprogge, 1989; Gibson, 1988, 1995; Rosenbloom & Way, 2004; Suárez-Orozco, 1989; Suárez-Orozco & Suáz-Orozco, 2001). In such contexts, immigrant parents value the educational opportunities migration offers their children and are therefore relatively tolerant toward discriminatory practices they and their children encounter (Gibson, 1988, 1995; Ogbu & Simons, 1998).

The group studied here, on the other hand, is confident about its past educational experience and imported skills, and sees them as relevant to education in their new environment. This stance is reinforced by the mystique of Soviet educational excellence, particularly in mathematics and the sciences, which has been prevalent in the West ever since the Sputnik revolution (King, 1973; Tomiak, 1986). The result is a rather confusing experience for their new teachers, most of whom are used to relating toward immigrant students from an assimilationist stance (see chapter 5 in this volume; Eisikovits, 1997; Gibson, 1997).

The teachers use the stereotype of the strong mathematician benevolently as an orienting concept. However, such stereotypical approaches are inherently depersonalizing. In this case, their damaging effect is felt most by Profile II informants, whose strengths lie in domains other than the scientific and mathematical.

Table 1.1. Youths' Position According to Profile Affiliation

Theme	General	Profile I	Profile II	Profile III
Immigration: Why and How	- Informants had no input in the decision to immigrate - Accepted unquestioningly parents' decision on their behalf in a matter of life-long consequence - Preimmigration preparation helped all informants cope better in the new setting - Unprepared informants of both genders experienced the cross-cultural transition as traumatic			
Schooling: Here and There	- Informants were reluctant to generalize about past school experience	- Perceived curricular tracking and diversified curriculum in the Israeli school as advantageous		- Viewed diversified curriculum in the new context as excluding them from real choices. They experienced their schooling in the present from a vantage point of disadvantage and idealized the past as a time of competence in their lives

Expectations from the new school	- Adopted a consumer conscious approach to their school and its staff. - Defined expectations on a personal level yet had a comparative overview of the workings of the two educational systems	- Had no clear expectations.
Attitude toward teachers	- Good teachers were considered an important "commodity" to be provided by the school. - Were most appreciative of treatment by teachers in the special NIS program.	- Felt highly susceptible to teacher attitudes.

Table continues on next page.

Table 1.1. Continued

Theme	General	Profile I	Profile II	Profile III
Career planning		- Most informants were male mathematics/science students. - Many attended specialized schools in the FSU. - They were well-informed about study options and career opportunities in the receiving society. - Had definite plans for higher education.	- Included mostly female informants. (a) Those few who stayed within their area of strength in the humanities and social sciences (many attended specialized schools in their home country) encountered opportunities for self-actualization in their new environment. (b) Those who were transferred to the mathematics/science track (the majority of informants) were discouraged by their negative experience. - They were not well informed about career opportunities and their future focused role image was blurred. - Recognized the importance of tertiary education, in general, but expressed doubts about their own ability to pursue such studies.	- Undecided - Had no specific plans

Attitude toward school-organized activities	- Considered them as unnecessary and even as cumbersome.	- Regarded the social integrative function of the school as crucial Accordingly, they were concerned about the isolative atmosphere of the NIS program and were interested in increasing the number of school initiated social activities.
Peer worlds: Distinct and separate.	- Distinguished between selected and circumstantial relationships, with a preference for same culture peers as personal friends. - Interpreted their low intensity relations with host country peers in reciprocal terms. Amplified intercultural variance to account for them.	- Same culture peers were perceived as a central social support system - Interpreted these relations as rejection by host country peers. Perceived their role as passively reacting to Sabra initiatives.
Immigrating during late adolescence	- Because scholastic adjustment was not seen as taxing, they considered this as good timing. It afforded the formation of a comparative perspective on experiences in the two systems.	- The challenge of personal social adjustment combined with he hardship of coping with requirements in a demanding new educational system were regarded as overpowering. Therefore this was viewed s a particularly problematic time for immigration.

Table continues on next page.

Table 1.1. Continued

Theme	General	Profile I	Profile II	Profile III
Who is an Israeli		- Adopted a pluralistic stance in asserting their national identity. - Preferred an additive approach toward social integration. Admitted their voluntary self-isolation accounted for by considerations of short-term convenience.	- Considered acceptance by mainstream society as preconditional for the assertion of their national identity.	
	- The army was perceived as a vehicle for social integration in the future.			

As shown, immigration has a differential impact on members of the three groups. Profile I informants who are mostly male, experienced immigration positively. They are an assertive group whose career planning process, a central mechanism of continued meaningful existence, has not been disturbed by immigration. These youths consciously employ cross-cultural adaptive strategies (Suárez-Orozco, 2004), They make choices from a position of competence in their various life spheres. The experience of Profile II and III interviewees is quite different.

Losses on the scholastic as well as the social level are greatest for the predominantly female group of Profile II informants, the *determined-affected*. Their life goals have been radically changed by immigration. They are confused about the future. The interviews reflect a decline in self-esteem and a passive self-perception in relations with host national peers and in general attitudes toward the host society. An individualized approach seems best suited for working with them. Flexible organizational frameworks will allow them to build on their original talents and will foster a sense of continuity in their personal and social identity. Their participation in intergroup contexts should be geared to bringing out their strengths, thus making possible the formation of more symmetrical relations with host culture peers.

Members of the *undecided* group experience the transition from a position of powerlessness in their relations with both school personnel and host culture peers. They, too, need intensive empowering socioeducational treatment to counterbalance the detrimental effect of lack of preparation in the country of origin and the trauma of cross-cultural migration. Both of these factors appear to have had the strongest impact on Profile III informants.

On the whole these immigrant youths shattered several premises of immigrant education policy and practice in their receiving society. They refuted the thesis of necessary interdependence between academic success and assimilation that used to be emphasized in the context of nation building (Kahane, 1986). Although intensive social integration may be central for younger age groups or NIS from other cultural backgrounds, the informants' preference for academic success de-emphasized the importance of the acculturative function of schools in Israeli society (See chapter 6 for a discussion of this topic). According to many, their teachers may have overdone rather than neglected "their social mission."

Members of this study population, along with other East European NIS, such as the Transylvanians, did not blindly accept the prevalent models of immigrant education. Instead, they reaffirmed the need for continuity in their lives. They made sense of the new school experience in light of their personal, family, and educational histories. Because they regarded the cultural endowment they brought with them as an asset, they insisted that it should be taken into account in further planning their education. Having had clearly formulated opinions on the role of the school and teachers, the informants expected to be consulted on the rate and extent of acculturative change to which they were willing to subscribe. In congruence with Gibson's (1988) approach of "accommodation without assimilation", they distinguished between short- and long-range social and educational goals and opted for gradual entry into the new society on negotiable rather than prescribed terms.

In this chapter 1 attempted to bring out the voices of these young immigrants on a variety of issues directly affecting their lives. The study should be considered part of the anthropological research trend that came to be known as the "ethnography of empowerment" (Ernst & Statzner, 1994; Fine, Burns, Payne, & Torre, 2004, 2007; McNeil, 2005; Nieto, 1999; Perry & Fraser, 1993; Spindler & Spindler, 1994). This group shares with other motivated and high-achieving immigrant student populations, such as the Transylvanians in Israel (Eisikovits, 1995c), the Chinese (Zhou, 1997), the Koreans (Sorensen, 1994) Central Americans (Suárez-Orozco, 1989) in the United States, a sense of family cohesion and parental support for academic effort. The assertiveness of the informants in this study and comparative critical approach toward the new educational environment, crucial factors in their educational success, stem from deep pride in their cultural heritage.

NOTES

1.   All names of informants, settings and localities have been altered to protect participants' anonymity.
2.   High scores on the matriculation exams in several subject matter areas are a prerequisite for admission to prestigious fields of study in all institutions of higher education.
3.   "Russia" was used broadly by the informants to refer to different parts of the FSU.
4.   Name of informants' town of residence in Transylvania.
5.   In the Former Soviet educational system the emphasis was on learning facts and oral testing (Muckle, 1990).
6.   Hebrew expression used to refer to native-born Israelis. The informants use it indiscriminately to cover all nonimmigrant Israeli youth.

CHAPTER 2

"IT IS OBVIOUS THAT GIRLS HAVE AN EASIER TIME"

Gender and Adaptation Style

As we have seen, academic adjustment of late-adolescent immigrants pointed to gender-based differences. Males with career plans in the sciences and mathematics had a relatively smooth academic transition into the new educational system, largely because the specializations of their choice were not heavily dependent on knowledge of the new language. In contrast, many of the females who originally planned careers in the social sciences and humanities had their plans considerably affected by immigration, because these were more culture-sensitive and language dependent. Thus, females had a more difficult time adjusting academically. In light of the above findings, I was interested in examining the social adjustment of late-adolescent immigrants from the Former Soviet Union, (FSU) with a particular emphasis on gender differences in social and cultural adaptation styles. While in the previous chapter profiles served as the analytic framework, here and in chapter four I consider gender-based responses to the challenges of migration and the style adopted to deal with them.

Studies on immigrant youth focus primarily on academic achievement (Gillborn & Gipps, 1996; Kao & Tienda, 1995; Lee, 1996; Suárez-Orozco,

Immigrant Youth Who Excel: Globalization's Uncelebrated Heroes, pp. 35–51
Copyright © 2008 by Information Age Publishing
All rights of reproduction in any form reserved.

2007; Zhou, 1997). As to the hard-to-assess issue of sociocultural adjustment, its normative manifestations are seldom addressed. The negative effects of lack of social adjustment, like truancy, drug abuse, delinquency, and other antisocial behaviors, are more salient categories in the social science research literature (Cohen, 1994; Eldering & Knorth, 1998; Feldman & Elliott, 1990; Ima, 1996; Nieto, 1995; Phelan, Davidson, & Yu, 1998; Valverde, 1987). The present study attempts to shed light on this largely neglected aspect of immigrant youths' cross-cultural transition. This topic captures the interest of researchers much less than outcome oriented categories of youths' adjustment, whether positive or negative. Throughout this book I seek to illustrate how important the existential experience, in other words, the process of adjustment, is, and how deeply it affects immigrant youths' performance in all realms of their involvement.

THE STUDY

This study group, like the one described in the previous chapter, also comprised 20 high school seniors (10 males and 10 females), aged 17–18, in Upper Hilltown. The only difference being that these informants immigrated at an earlier age (12–13 rather than 15–16) and had spent 4 to 5 years in Israel (as opposed to only 1 to 2 years) at the time of the interviews, enabling me to consider long-term effects of migration.

Data collection consisted of in-depth interviews, supplemented by ongoing participant observation in various in-school and out-of-school settings frequented by the informants. I carried out most of the interviews in single 2-hour sessions in the school lounge which is located in a relatively quiet corner of the building. We met after school with both time and place selected by the individual informants with the assistance of one of the teachers who helped me coordinate the scheduling.[1] The room was decorated in lively colors and was comfortably furnished with armchairs and coffee tables conducive to creating a relaxed and informal atmosphere. In these encounters I followed the guidelines of the ethnographic interview, whereby I informed participants of the purpose of the study and the main issues to be addressed; however, I gave them the freedom to answer as they saw fit (Flick, 2006; Wolcott, 1995). The interviews focused on four main topics: their perceptions of the social role of the school in bringing new immigrants and veteran or native Israelis closer together; attitudes toward friendship with same- and host-culture peers; views on dating same- and host-culture partners (in heterosexual relationships); and their notions of what a desirable style of accommodation is.

The informants enjoyed hearing about my longstanding research interest in the cultural adjustment of immigrant youths and consequently felt comfortable to use the interviews as an opportunity to both formulate their positions and reflect upon them. Many did not have distinct views because they lacked contexts for opinion formation. In their family they seldom have the occasion to talk about such matters. From our conversations it became apparent that typically there is little intergenerational exchange of ideas in these families—a finding which is in line with the contention of scholars who had described the Soviet and post-Soviet family climate, such as Bronfenbrenner (1970) and more recently Pearson (1990) and Markowitz (2000). This explains the empowering effect of the interviews as rare opportunities to talk about issues of vital importance to them with an adult and accounts for their degree of openness to discuss with me often delicate matters.

THE SCHOOL'S SOCIAL FUNCTION

Attitudes towards the potential role of school are colored by the informants' imported conceptions. School was an important arena for their activity in Russia and expectations from it are also high in the country of migration. As teenagers, the school is the one central social institution with which they are well acquainted and consequently feel confident to express their opinion about.

A strong gender-based difference is apparent in their perceptions. Whereas male informants tend to see the primary role of school as academic, rejecting attempts at social integration, females are more apt to recognize that school is virtually their only meeting ground with host-culture peers and with Israeli society in general. Thus, males assume a more separatist approach and females a more integrationist attitude.

The "official" isolationist male position, characteristic of the academically successful students, referred to as Profile I in chapter one, is voiced by Oleg:

> All I want to learn in school is electronics. The social stuff is unimportant. Ask all the new immigrant students. In the future I will only remember the important things, such as electronics, that I learnt there. Look, now in school I am in an integrated class, right? Who do I spend my time with? Twenty percent with Israelis and eighty percent with Russian kids. During the breaks we [the Russian immigrants] are together all the time.

An even more extreme separatist stance is adopted by some of the weaker male students in the study group. Igor exclaims:

> Why not have separate classes for *Olim* (new immigrants) so we can speak freely among ourselves? Russian kids understand each other. When I first said something in class they laughed at me. Ever since, I keep my mouth shut in class, as if I'm not even there.

On the whole, males reject school-initiated integrative efforts as artificial. Boris explains: "Nothing is worse than forcing these 'friendships.' Let things happen by themselves. Time will take care of it. Kids react badly to such pressure." Males tend to be reticent towards school activities aimed at enhancing intergroup rapprochement, as they feel it only underlines their inferiority. In fact, they go as far as justifying veteran or *Sabra* peers for refusing to take on the task of actively ushering in their new immigrant classmates. Boris continues: "Why should *Sabra*s bother to be so friendly with us? They have their own group since childhood. So it's only natural that we live in two separate worlds." By rejecting the role of the Israeli school in social integration, many of the male informants deproblematize ethnic enclosure, portraying it as a self-elected option.

The only way the male informants envision in-school social integration to be possible is on the basis of their own academic strength and its recognition by their veteran Israeli schoolmates. Vladimir remarks with an ironic smile: "Once they realized they could get help from me in math, physics or chemistry, I became 'desirable company.' " Thus, academic success is perceived to be a precondition for social acceptance. This *emic* (insiders') position is contradictory to the tenet held in the literature whereby school performance of immigrant and minority students is contingent upon their social adjustment and upon their ability to overcome structural barriers in school (Gillborn, 1997; Kahane, 1986; Ogbu & Simons, 1998; van Zanten, 1997; Zhou, 1997, 2003). Though valid for low achievers, this contention does not seem to hold for these high achievers who disregard the school's socializing role.

Several males think that integration between immigrant and veteran youth is best served by immersion in total life situations, such as in the course of compulsory military service. They prefer a "no choice" approach to social adjustment. Igor clarifies: "There (in the army) you will have to become part of things. You can't run home to your friends and parents. Also, when peoples' lives depend on each other, that draws them together automatically."

A characteristic salient in several of the males' responses is the use of various forms of disassociation between personal belief and a range of normative positions on the school's social mission. This is a stylistic device which provides the user with a convenient cop-out from committal statements. Ilia, a particularly eloquent informant, illustrates it:

I can see that school takes on the role of educator. It is not only a provider of knowledge. However, I don't see myself participating in any of this stuff. It can only work in the guise of fun, if school can manage to do things the fun way, without kids suspecting it's for a cause. Zionism, Communism, it's all propaganda. Kids hate it.

Along similar lines, Dima states that "the school takes its responsibility of absorbing new immigrant students seriously," but avoids voicing his opinion, which he was asked for. Boris offers an extreme response of distancing: "How should I know, I am just a student! What right do I have to say what school should do in addition to teaching students?" His sense of disempowerment—as a stranger to the country and as a young person reared in an adult-oriented society (Markowitz, 1996; Pearson, 1990)—is so pervasive that he does not feel entitled to a position of his own.

By and large, males are more critical of Israeli schools than females. After 4 or 5 years in their new society, they still compare them with Russian schools, idealizing the former. Being critical of Israeli schools, or rather being able to criticize school, may be empowering at a time when many of them feel at such a low ebb. Although males reject the social function of the school, it is evident they lack alternative sources for learning about their receiving society. By diminishing the acculturative function of the school while emphasizing its information-providing role, they reduce their chances of obtaining cultural literacy. This, in turn, has a disempowering effect on their lives, leading to their further marginalization.

In sharp contrast, females attribute much more importance to the school's social role. They tend to be more interested in careers in the social sciences and humanities, for which cultural literacy is more important. They discuss their continued ethnic enclosure candidly, as endangering their future, and actively seek ways to break out of it.

Females regard school as the major setting for getting to know host-culture peers. "To this day all the Israelis I know I have met through school," Alina says. Hence, they favor the school's deliberate intervention in bridging between cultures. Alina adds:

School shouldn't leave new immigrant students together in big groups in one class even if the *Olim* are afraid. At first they may be afraid, but then they start mixing with the *Sabras*. Without such steps we will stay stuck on the sideline and feel like we're living in a different country.

Females see Israeli peers as more powerful ("They know the rules, it's their country"), and use their own powerlessness as leverage, equating it with femininity. They take a passive view of themselves and expect to be treated chivalrously by host-culture peers, who, in their view, should show interest in new immigrant students and initiate intergroup rapprochement in school.

WHO IS A FRIEND

As Russian parents are preoccupied with their own existential struggles, the young immigrants are more or less left to themselves and their same-culture peers to sort out their problems. The lack of family involvement in the lives of teenagers has a twofold effect: it engenders unclarity about future directions and generates a feeling that parents cannot serve as a source of guidance in the new context. Suárez-Orozco (1989, 1995) also comments on family unavailability to support the psycho-social integration of adolescents in his study of Central American refugees in the United States. This enhances youths' isolation and sense of ineffectiveness. At the same time, it reinforces the importance of the same-culture peer group as a primary support system. The Transylvanians present a unique case in this respect, in that parental support was, according to the informants, made available to them throughout their process of cross-cultural accommodation. This was particularly important due to the fact that this group of immigrants scattered in the new country, making access to same culture peers problematic.

Informants categorize their peers into Russians and Israelis. Friends and friendship are classified accordingly as a reflection of the way they perceive their universe to be divided. "Friendship," denoting the highest degree of proximity or intimacy in dyadic relations, is reserved for the intimate clique of initiates, all of whom are same-culture peers. Within this sheltered milieu, the immigrants talk about feelings, process their isolation and strangeness in the new society: "We can talk about everything because we understand and trust each other. These are real friends; a real friend won't hurt or harm you under any condition," says Igor. The fact that friendship is assessed in terms of maintenance of one's personal safety may be an expression of the informants' intense sense of vulnerability. It also signals these youths' dire need for a sense of security these intense relations offer.

In contrast, when characterizing their relationships with same-sex Israeli peers, "friendship" does not come up; the term is not perceived as relevant by informants of either gender. Talking about his veteran classmates who are the only Israelis he knows, Ilia says: "They are neither my friends nor my enemies. These are people I meet in school and sometimes on the street. We respect each other." As to the emotional climate in these intercultural peer relations, Vadim explains: "I don't love or hate them. I accept them. The differences are just too big and too many."

When asked to explain or specify these differences, none of the participants can come up with anything specific.

Out-of-school contacts with host-culture peers are limited to accidental meetings at the shopping center, movies or sports facilities. "I've never planned an outing with an Israeli kid," Vladimir remarks. The topics of conversation are superficial, activity- or context-related. Indeed, informants of both genders exhibit considerable ignorance regarding the lifestyle and daily routine of their host-culture age mates and basic factual knowledge about their country of migration in general. Since intercultural contact is minimal, they are seldom called upon to explain these disparities to critical audiences. In discussions with same-culture peers, the differences are taken for granted and used as slogans or ritual utterances that function as consensus-building devices. Part of the informants' creed is that one cannot simultaneously have friends from both groups. "It's like two blocs and you have to choose between them," Dima explains. Interviewees often present in-group relations as too precious to abandon for the sake of intergroup contacts with veteran Israelis—a polarized world view of total belonging versus mutual exclusion characteristic of teenagers in which simultaneous membership is unthinkable.

While males present their homogeneous same-culture peer group as a matter of choice, among females one can hear voices that admit, as Clarissa does, that the situation is imposed on them: "Some say they prefer their Russian friends, but I say I only met other new immigrant kids in the *Ulpan*, in school and in most other places. You understand, these are the only kids I could make friends with."

WHOM TO DATE

The topic of courtship is closely related to the informants' musings about friendship, as is the issue of romantic partners from the same or host culture. As their life is divided into in-group and out-group, into intimate and strange, courtship, gender relations and models of femininity and masculinity are similarly viewed through this prism.

Males depend on the Russian group for both same-sex and cross-sex relations. Hence, their belonging to the culture of origin is more absolute. Females, on the other hand, may envision the configuration of same-sex friendship within the ethnic peer-group and concomitant romantic ties with host-culture peers. However, the presence of the same-culture confidante is considered key to meaningful existence, creating a counterbalance with the Israeli male friend, indeed an identity anchor. Irina explains: "I can't imagine my life without my Russian girlfriend. She opens her heart to me, she takes me real seriously. I can be on the phone with her for hours. She will always make time for me and give me genuine advice." It took both time and a shift in analytic perspective on my part as researcher, to reexamine these cultural inclinations, first construed as isolationist, from a transnationalist viewpoint, along with the development of the latter as an alternative frame of reference to the study of immigrant adaptation patterns (Brettell, 2000; Glick-Schiller, Basch, Blanc-Szanton, 1995; Lewellen, 2002).

Most females categorize this relationship with the same-sex, same-culture confidante as "friendship," in comparison to which the cross-cultural courtship is seen as an ancillary relationship which pays utilitarian dividends, easing their way into the new society. This duality makes it possible to keep one foot in each world. The same-culture confidante, in addition to her experience-processing function, may also be instrumental in making the foray into the "opposite camp" more acceptable by ethnic peer-group standards.

Both genders have highly traditional stereotypical sex-role attitudes which color their views on the role of courtship and the desirability of cross-cultural romantic ties.[2] For example, it is commonly agreed that when going on a date, the male has to pay for the outing. "This is the custom, it is a sign of manhood. The boy pays as an act of chivalry to show the date was his initiative," Marina clarifies. This attitude gives immigrant females an advantage over males in terms of finding an Israeli courtship partner. As Sandra puts it: "It is obvious that girls have an easier time. It is not their role to initiate so they are less likely to be rejected. If I were a boy I wouldn't risk asking an Israel girl out. Who wants to be ridiculed?"

In contrast, females see Israeli males in a favorable position: "Why should they hesitate to strike up a conversation with a Russian girl?" asks Katia, and she goes on: "They know they are in charge. If they get a refusal, it won't hurt them too much." These females treat the Israelis as a uniform social entity whose knowledge of the rules bestows on them an aura of omnipotence.

Since it is commonplace that courtship is initiated by them, the male informants do not feel confident to take such forward action towards Israeli females because of their earlier mentioned powerlessness. This, however, is not overtly acknowledged. Instead they fault host-culture females for being "too aggressive," and, as such, not conforming to their ideal of femininity. Igor brings the following incident to illustrate this claim: "Once I tried to open a car door for a *Sabra* girl, as I am used to. Her reaction was: 'Do I look incapable of opening the door for myself?' Who would want to ask a girl like that for a date?"

While most males think that, in principle, cross-cultural dating can be a good way in to the host-culture peer group, they seldom envision it as a real option for themselves. Alex claims: "I have nothing to talk about with an

Israeli girl. With a Russian girl I can talk about everything on heaven and earth." Oleg concurs: "Why should an Israeli girl want to go out with a new immigrant without a car, who can't take her to fancy places?" It is not only a matter of low self-image. These young men distrust the host culture, which inherently rules out the possibility of mixed dating. Intimate relationships with partners with whom one has no cultural and existential affinity are inconceivable.

Males agree that their female counterparts have an easier time: "For Russian girls, such relationships are a golden opportunity," says Arcadi, "They are pretty so the Israeli boys like them. They don't have to be afraid of refusals." Yet, males see females' preference for cross-cultural dating as an act of betrayal. Vladimir remarks: "They should stick with their own kind. But regardless of that, is it possible to get emotional support from a stranger?" He dismisses the females who prefer this option, as "they are the cheap sort, anyway," and adds ironically "such relationships are based on money, not on love."

Females' views on this matter vary. Some consider mixed courtship as a means for mutual cultural learning. Katia says: "It is important for me to learn about their lifestyle and for them to learn about mine." Larissa expands: "How else will I break out of the Russian ghetto?" She goes on: "It's a challenge. Besides, Russian boys don't dress cool and are not attractive." But for a few females, such intercultural relationships become traps. "Israeli boyfriends sometimes lock you in an exclusive tie which holds you back instead of opening up possibilities to meet new people," Marina explains. An instrumental attitude toward such relationships is apparent in these accounts. However, a small number expressed preference for same-culture courtship as the more rewarding alternative.

Regardless of the cultural affiliations of present male friend or female friend, preference for future marriage partners points in the direction of the same-culture contingent. The reason offered by female as well as male informants is the optimal condition for consensual child rearing that it provides. They plan to raise their children in the spirit of the country of origin, which indicates long-term identification with it, corroborating theories upholding long-term ethnic adhesion tendencies of these immigrants (Al-Haj, 2002; Remennick, 2007).

TWO WAYS TO ADJUST

The final topic explored, unemphasized in immigration studies of youths, is how participants experience their own integration into the new society. In the interviews, adjustment emerged as a crucial element in their lives. However, the informants have uncrystallized views on it, which could be interpreted as a measure of their bewilderment by the issues involved. This becomes conspicuous through comparison with other topics on which they have well defined ideas (such as friends and friendship, dating and courtship). The reason might also be that the latter are more age-appropriate concerns, whereas integration and adjustment are complex abstract categories that evoke their sense of impotence vis-à-vis a general-ized notion of the receiving society.

Informants use the interview as an opportunity to clarify their position on this topic to themselves and the interviewer. While they are unable to conceptualize cross-cultural adjustment or provide succinct profiles of adjusted individuals, they exhibit remarkable awareness of their own adaptive course. They are able to reconstruct their priorities and their shifting emphases on a time line in the different spheres of their lives (e.g., school and studies, investment in the acquisition of language skills, friends and friendship). Thus, they exhibit a self-reflective longitudinal perspective on their own experience.

One of the factors strongly linked to adjustment, particularly in the ini-tial stages, is knowledge of the host-country language. The importance of the new language and its acquisition usually come up in a social context—as a facilitator or hindrance to intercultural communication. Sergey explains:

> Without the language [Hebrew], I felt at first like a deaf, dumb and blind person, then only dumb like a dog who understands but can't say anything. Everyone has to go through these phases, but they better not last too long. It's bad for the ego.

Language and friendship with same- or host-culture peers are tightly con-nected topics. For females, language acquisition and friends hold highest priority at the incipient phases of their cross-cultural migration (Cam-eron, 1998). Lena elaborates "My old friends were left behind. I needed to make new ones because I never was without friends." Most of them decided that same-culture peers were better candidates for "new friends," not only because of the common experience base but also because of the acutely felt language barrier vis-à-vis host-culture peers.

The interviewees see language ability as a primary adaptation marker (or a barrier thereof) without taking mutual intergroup perceptions into account. This shortcoming can be ascribed either to social ignorance or to denial of their rejection by host-culture peers. Lack of effective language skills allows for an explanation of communication failure on an "objec-tive" or factual level, without loss of face—a strategy more prevalent among the males.

The issue of adjustment was interpreted differently by the two genders. Males regard themselves as adapting to an environment which is primarily physical—a locale rather than an entity with a distinct social dimension. They interpret adjustment on a more technical level, as being able to orient themselves in their new country. Adopting a spectator rather than a participant stance, Ilia explains: "To be adjusted means you are not a stranger. You understand what is going on. You know the language, can communicate and don't consider yourself being apart from your surroundings." Vadim elaborates:

> We share the same space but I don't want to become part of the Israeli group. We prefer our own circle and they prefer theirs. It's O.K. to live side by side. I learnt the language quite well, I can get around. I like the country and don't need Israeli friends to consider myself adjusted.

Females, in contrast, interpret adjustment as a social process, one that includes Israeli peers as a necessary audience to confirm its success. They tend to use more descriptors of individual emotions, stressing how acculturation makes them feel. Females talk about themselves as more adjustment oriented and willing to change. They describe Russian males as shy, passive, not ready to make efforts for social adjustment, unwilling to risk rejection, hiding in their own closed world. Alina specifies: "They forget it's us who came to their country, not they to ours. It's really up to us to try to fit in. Instead the boys try to turn Upper Hilltown into Little Ukraine."

It is noteworthy that after 4 or 5 years in their new country, females still maintain a strong group identity, using "us" versus "them" rhetoric throughout the interviews while criticizing the males for their isolationist views. Indeed, like the males, they use expressions that distance themselves, that depict experiences from the outside. Sandra defines adjustment as follows: "An adjusted person is someone who no longer lives in a closed world, has Israeli friends, accepts the way of life here"; Irina calls someone adjusted when "He or she has no problem connecting with Israelis, knows the language, feels at ease in conversation with Israelis." In fact, participants of both genders use an impersonal mode when referring to the characteristics of the adjusted individual as "someone who found his or her place" or "a person who doesn't search any more." Wary of declarations, they avoid speaking from personal experience or using first-person narration in spite of their self-reflective approach.

They use their cultural uniqueness as an armor, even though group activities are not necessarily culturally based. Arcadi clarifies: "We don't talk about Tolstoy or Dostoyevski all day long, but about regular day-to-day stuff. Still, when we are among ourselves we don't need to explain everything. No need for lots of words." Phrases like "we are different," "we have a different mentality," "we have different interests" abound in their discourse, but their value is declarative (to enhance group cohesiveness) rather than substantive. The male informants are aware of the asymmetry of power relations with *Sabras* but lack the competencies to alter the imbalance.

When discussing their future, males project themselves in terms of their career and personal life goals and try to minimize their context dependence. Career orientation is stronger among young males, who report having devoted more effort to academic school learning than females in the first stages of transition. When future goals entail a change of professional direction (mainly among females), informants interpret this as stemming from personal reasons, such as shifts in areas of interest or realistically assessed changes in perceptions of their own ability. Lara says: "At the age of twelve or thirteen kids don't have plans for the future. They have fantasies to be prime minister, a pilot, a journalist or a movie star." Katia adds: "Once I was good in science, now I prefer literature and the humanities. To be a good mathematician I would have to put in a lot of effort. Literature is more interesting than solving math problems." This attitude diverges from that voiced by participants in the previous study, reported upon in chapter 1, which attributed deviation from their original plans to the impact of immigration and who usually perceived such changes as having a negative effect on their identity and self-worth.

Table 2.1 provides a gender-based summary of the informants' main positions on the topics discussed. It also presents some cross-gender patterns and stylistic characteristics that emerge from the interviews.

CONCLUDING REMARKS

Examining the issue of social adjustment among high school seniors who had immigrated from the FSU, this study complements the one reported upon in chapter one. It was carried out with a similar group of informants (same country of origin, age range and location in Israel), with one exception: the age at which they immigrated and the length of time in the host country. Whereas the group dealt with in the first study had arrived in Israel at the age of 15–16, only 1–2 years prior to the research, the one in the present study had immigrated at 12–13 years and had already spent 4–5 years in Israel at the time of the interviews. While the first study investigated academic adjustment and the second probed social adaptation, the consistency of attitudes between the two is high. Both study groups saw the school's main role as instrumental (academic) rather than

Table 2.1. Youth Views According to Gender

Theme	Cross-Gender Characteristics	Males' Views	Females' Views
The school's social function		- See the academic role of the school as its primary function - Reject school-initiated integrative efforts as artificial. - Believe only possibility for social integration in school is on the basis of demonstrated academic strength. - Prefer enhancement of inter-group relations through total life situations, such as in the course of military service, where they believe rapprochement will occur by itself.	- Recognize that school is their main meeting ground with host culture peers. - Support school's deliberate intervention in bridging between cultures
Who is a friend	- The term "friend" is not applied to host-culture peers - Considerable ignorance regarding the lifestyle and daily routine of the host-culture peer group—both cause and effect of their isolation.	- Portray homogeneous same-culture peer group as a matter of choice.	- Admit scarcity of opportunities to meet host-culture peers informally. Hence, friendship with same-culture peers is seen as an outcome of circumstances rather than a matter of choice.
Whom to date	- Hold traditional stereotypical sex-role attitudes (e.g., the male has to pay during a date).	- Depend on the in-group for both same-sex and cross-gender relations. Hence, their belonging to the culture of origin is more absolute	- Can hold simultaneous same-sex friendships within the "Russian" group and romantic ties with host-culture peers. Define the same-culture relationships as more meaningful

Table continues on next page.

Table 2.1. Continued

Theme	Cross-Gender Characteristics	Males' Views	Females' Views
		- Can see advantages to cross-cultural dating in principle, but don't consider it a feasible option for themselves. Distrust members of the receiving society, which rules out the possibility of establishing such relationships.	- Some regard intergroup courtship as an opportunity for mutual learning, an entry into the host-culture peer world. Most maintain an instrumental attitude towards such relationships.
Two ways to adjust	- Consider acquisition of new language a crucial factor in facilitating or hindering intergroup communication.	- Interpret adjustment on the level of technical orientation skills.	- Relate to the emotional effects of adjustment.
	- Use impersonal mode of reporting when describing characteristics of the adjusted individual (rather than relating to personal experience).	- Perceive adjustment in a spatial context.	- Feel that adjustment is necessarily a social process.
	- Their world is clearly divided into same-culture and host-culture peers.	- Largely separatist approach towards host culture. Use their cultural uniqueness as a shielding mechanism.	- Hold more integrationist attitudes. Consider host-culture peers an important audience in the process of identity formation in the context of their cross-cultural transition.
	- In relating to host-culture peers, a "we" identity is applied.	- Project themselves into the future in terms of their personal career goals, thereby minimizing their context dependence.	- Plan careers mostly in the humanities and social sciences, which are markedly culture dependent.
		- Interpret attitude of host-culture peers to immigrant youths as a group or class rather than an individual phenomenon (less threatening).	- Perceive relationships with host-culture peers as also dependent on the efforts immigrant youths are willing to invest.
		- Report having emphasized academic success and career goals at initial stages of cross-cultural migration.	- Report having emphasized language acquisition and the establishment of new friendships to replace friends left behind during the first months of arrival.

social, particularly males; and both groups felt more comfortable with same-culture peers and had little contact with veteran Israelis outside the classroom.

This consistency can be attributed to a lack of compartmentalization of life events. Age at immigration and time spent in the receiving society, held to be important parameters influencing scholastic as well as social adjustment of young immigrants (Gibson, 1995; Rumbaut, 1995), do not seem to have much impact on the informants in these studies. This is probably because the above claim stems from an assimilationist paradigm, whereas the immigrant group in question (particularly the males) consciously opts for a transnationalist approach in their style of adaptation.

These two sequential studies allow us to consider patterns of change and persistence in the perceptions and attitudes of these youngsters. By talking to informants, one gains an understanding of how they experience their own transition and how they incorporate it into their emergent identities. As these processes occur simultaneously, they co-constitute each other. Though room has to be made for individual differences, there are extensive similarities between the two study groups, both of which exhibit high intragroup uniformity.

In comparison with the informants interviewed in the previous project, the present group is much less future- and career-oriented, but rather more preoccupied with their experiences in the present, age-appropriate concerns with their social life. Nonetheless, academic success is still considered very important and the only basis on which males can envision the establishment of social rapport with veteran youngsters in school on a more balanced ground. This stance is in opposition to mainstream research on immigrant students' school performance, for which adaptation to the school climate in the receiving society is considered preconditional (Abedi, 2004; Gillborn, 1997; Pang, 2006; van Zanten, 1997).

In spite of the younger age at the time of their arrival (early as opposed to late adolescence) the members of this group (particularly males) are still largely inward directed and have not relinquished their "we" identity. They are only marginally influenced by the host society models of adolescent behavior and cross-sex relations. Ideals of gender identity are sought in the culture of origin and are used as reactive boundary-maintaining devices.

As a result of the intercultural distance, ignorance about the day-to-day reality of life in the host society after 5 years is conspicuously high. Although participants live in a town relatively isolated from metropolitan centers, the small size of the country puts these centers within their easy reach. Indeed, interviewees report frequenting their amusement sites and teenager hang-outs regularly. However, this is done as a group activity.

These outings are not seen as occasions for intergroup mingling, particularly not by males.

The findings reveal an underlying theme of powerlessness among immigrant males and females alike. However, each gender experiences and describes the feeling behind the theme differently, sensing it at various degrees of acuteness. The data indicate that females can more readily function on the basis of conscious powerlessness. They talk about it more freely and treat it pragmatically as a transitory hurdle which is therefore seen as surmountable. This renders them better skilled at cultural "border crossing" (Phelan, Davidson, & Yu, 1993). They desire to establish ongoing transactions with veteran Israeli youths and incorporate lessons learned from them in their conscious acculturation.

Spindler and Spindler (1993) make a distinction between the "enduring self," meaning one's sense of continuity with the past, and the "situated self," or the contextualized aspects of the person, which is pertinent here. As demonstrated throughout this chapter, females' higher self-awareness of their own adaptive course prepares them to function effectively on the level of the situated self without jeopardizing their enduring self.

Males, on the other hand, have more difficulty with the situation. They cannot envisage themselves functioning from a subordinate position vis-à-vis peers in the receiving society. They deal with this by retreating to the in-group and keeping informal social interaction with host-culture peers to a minimum, using self-alienation as a shielding mechanism. By remaining rooted to their culture of origin and confining their activity to the ethnic sphere, males' feeling of competence is increased. However, these dividends are limited to the immediate future and have a marginalizing effect in the long run.

This study clearly indicates that in the perception of these immigrant youths' intergroup collaboration is only possible if and when mutually negotiated. In other words, the cohesive same-culture peer group and ethnic identification, in general, provide the stamina necessary for cross-cultural interaction. It also highlights the fact that this energy is limited and only allows for partial, rather than full, participation in selected contexts.

Shaw (1994) maintains that in order to develop a sense of identity, identification with a moral community whose members share definitions of core values is essential. This group of immigrant youths constitutes such a moral community. Its male and female members express varying degrees of ambivalence regarding their exclusive belonging to it. Males manifest a more absolute long-term commitment anchored in Russian identity, whereas females exhibit more of a transitional identity, and are torn between loyalty and attraction to the two peer worlds.

Throughout this study females disclose higher globalization fitness. They are more open and adjustable, command better language skills, although their career choices, as shown in the previous chapter, tend to be more locally oriented. Whereas males are less territorially bound and more globally oriented in their career preferences. However, cultural defensiveness counteracts their intentions to develop globalist future focused role images. Chances are that in a more reciprocal, culturally balanced scenario they would be in an improved position to make their assets work.

NOTES

1. The author is indebted to Niza Allon for her assistance in coordinating the interviews.
2. It should be noted that, in the 1980s, a massive educational campaign was launched in the U.S.S.R. to promote traditional sex-role behavior. This was in reaction to the reduction of normative behavioral differences between the sexes brought about by the Communist ideal of gender equality (Attwood, 1990), which resulted, according to Soviet psychologists, in a drop in birth rates to the point that it had demographic consequences.

CHAPTER 3

"DEMOCRACY IS MORE FUN"

Voting in a New Political Culture

A vast amount of research has been conducted on political socialization
(Claussen & Mueller, 2000; Niemi, Hepburn, & Chapman, 2000; Torney-
Purta, 2000, 2002), citizenship education (Galston, 2001, 2004; Gifford,
2004; Hess, 2002; Ichilov, 1998; Haste, 2004; Torney-Purta, 2004; Yates &
Youniss, 1999), the development of political attitudes (Ichilov, 2003; Ross,
2004; Sherrod, 2004), and orientations toward democracy and civic activity (Blair, 2004; Flanagan, 2003; Hollis, 2004; Ichilov, Bar-Tal, & Mazawi,
1989; Milner, 2002; Niemi, Hepburn, & Chapman, 2000; Westheimer &
Kahne, 2004; Shumer & Belbas, 1996). By contrast, the literature on the
disposition of youth toward elections and voting is limited (Eisikovits,
Hedin, & Adam, 1984; Wilkinson, 1996). Although immigrant youngsters
constitute an ever-growing share of youthful populations in a globalized
world (Stepick & Stepick, 2002), their views on the topic have not been
studied. Extant research mainly comprises surveys of various immigrant
groups' party affiliations and voting patterns with no differentiation as to
participants' age groups, lumping together youths with adults.

The study I report about in this chapter explores the position of a
group of immigrant youths from the European republics of the Former
Soviet Union (FSU) on participation in public life in Israel, as expressed
in attitudes to voting in the 1996 national elections. Having immigrated

as young adolescents during the early 1990s, this was the first election in which they were eligible to take part, as they reached the minimum voting age of 18. The previous two chapters that dealt with cultural adaptation styles, indicated an inclination toward limited involvement in the broader social affairs of the receiving society and a preference for gradual integration, specifically in areas of direct personal interest, such as academic achievement and career planning. This orientation was paralleled by the young immigrants' tendency to isolate themselves within the secure boundaries of their own cultural peer group in social gatherings and leisure activities of their choice. The above disposition is in sharp contrast with that described by Stepick and Stepick (2002) for the United States, concerning immigrant youth's rapid Americanization and Portes and Rumbaut's (2001) claim with regard to their preference for English. Young persons in this study preferred to use their mother tongue whenever situationally appropriate, regardless of the amount of time spent in the receiving country. The present study proposed to analyze the attitudes of this group of relatively low political involvement in a period preceding elections, which is generally characterized by a preoccupation with public affairs and the urge to shape the future of one's society (Eisikovits, Hedin, & Adam, 1984).

In a comparative study of the outlook on elections of young Americans and Israelis who are native-born or long-time residents, several parameters were related to a positive approach to participating in the ballot (Eisikovits, Hedin, & Adam, 1984): feelings of being affected by the larger political system and of being able to affect it; practice and skills in administration and decision making at the school, youth organization, or community level; experience in such indirect political activity as volunteer service and community improvement projects; involvement in school-based educational programs aimed at solving social problems; perception of voting as a significant rite of passage to adulthood; and evaluation of candidates as deserving representatives of their constituencies. Although this research was carried out more than 2 decades ago, most of these parameters, indicative of active involvement and empowerment, inherent to the democratic process itself, can be expected to continue to reflect the position of youngsters in both societies today.

Political scientists deplore the low level of interest in elections and politics in general as well as the dearth of information on democratic practices and institutions among youngsters in Western Europe (Van Deth, Maraffi, Newton, & Whiteley, 1999) and the United States (Galston, 2001; Milner, 2002). Examining Israeli teenagers' perspectives on democracy, Ichilov et al. (1989) found that native-born and long-time residents had difficulty understanding the meaning of democracy and applying democratic precepts to solving social controversies. These researchers concluded that students from higher socioeconomic background showed a better comprehension of democratic concepts than respondents from lower socioeconomic background. Those with a lower socioeconomic status were more likely to describe their parents as uninvolved in politics and reported an absence of family discussion about such matters. Given the different political culture that the immigrant youths and their families experienced in their country of origin, this study examines and compares their outlooks on voting and political participation with those of native-born Israeli and long-time resident groups.

According to Torney-Purta (2000), much of the research on political socialization from the 1960s to the 1980s concentrated on assessing the impact of various sources of influence on the process, but this emphasis is no longer common because of its strictly linear logic. Nonetheless, to grasp the political attitudes of immigrant adolescents in cross-cultural transition, the effect of forces in the culture of origin and in the receiving society on the formation of political opinions must be comparatively explored. The research importance of the cultural-historical and personal context within which political socialization takes place is highlighted by Sigel (1995). This line of inquiry also emphasizes the centrality of sources of influence, one of the focuses of the present study.

Niemi, Hepburn, and Chapman (2000) maintain that research on political socialization should concentrate on the period when youths approach adult-like learning capacities rather than on earlier ages. Participants in this study were on the verge of operationalizing their political rights through voting, so the connection between political socialization and action is unequivocal.

Immigrants from the FSU, although granted full citizen rights in Israel, consider themselves as de-territorialized "Russians," creating a transnational space in their new country. Whereas in the country of origin they saw themselves as members of a persecuted Jewish minority, once in Israel the original cultural linkages grew stronger in adults as well as in youths, as I have shown in chapter two. In this chapter I examine whether these emotions were present in the immigrant youngsters' perceptions of their civic (as opposed to personal) identity and how they came to expression. Kearney (1995) notes that the scope of international migration has brought about the replacement of the concept of culture, as a cornerstone of anthropological research, by the more dynamic notion of identity.

In their previous environment, immigrant youths, like their elders, developed a code of conduct in which civic identity was disregarded because the state and its representative bureaucratic structures were considered oppressors of individual rights and needs. This engendered an overall distrust of officialdom, which made loyalty to political ideologies absurd (Horowitz, 1994). This study considers how their sceptical approach to politics and politicians affected attitudes to elections and governance in the new country.

THE STUDY

Information about the study was presented to the immigrant students by their civics teachers. Thirty 18-year-old high-school seniors, 14 males and 16 females, from three public high schools in the Northern City metropolitan area volunteered to participate. The informants' interest in the study was stimulated by the reported lack of opportunities to discuss their views with Israelis, Israeli adults in particular, outside the school setting. Therefore participants valued the opportunity for exchange and found the experience of having their opinions considered seriously, empowering. Some noted that the interview enhanced the formulation of their positions on the election.

Informants were interviewed in April, preceding the May 1996 general elections.[1] Four open-ended pilot interviews were conducted with participants selected for their high level of interest in public affairs and verbal competence based on recommendations of their civics teachers. These four students (two males and two females), not included in the group of 30 participants, also volunteered to take part in the study for reasons similar to those of the larger group. In the pilot interviews the immigrant youths were encouraged to discuss in detail and in an unstructured format their views on the political system in their country of migration and their civic involvement. The purpose of the pilot interviews was to allow these key informants to map out the field of knowledge and assist in the preparation of a comprehensive culturally informed ethnographic interview guide. From the content analysis of these pilot interviews four central themes emerged: civic identity, comparison of the two political systems, sources of influence on voting (school, the media, family, peers), and expectations of change as a result of the elections.

The semistructured interviews (Wolcott, 1995, 1999) applied to the larger study group addressed these four large topics. In these interviews the participants were asked to relate only to the topics that emerged from the analysis of the pilot interviews. This limitation of scope enabled systematic collection of data on the four central topics.

All interviews, recorded and transcribed, were conducted in school lobbies, cafes, and participants' homes, according to their preferences. The open-ended interviews lasted 2 hours; the semistructured ones lasted 1 hour on average. All interviewees had lived in Israel 5 to 6 years at the time of the research and had migrated at the age of 12 or 13. Information about the participants' socioeconomic profiles, collected as part of the informal conversations preceding the interviews, was used to interpret the data.

The interviews clearly indicated that informants differed considerably in their political knowledge base, their interest to participate in civic affairs, and the importance they attached to the elections as an expression of that interest. According to these parameters, three types of attitudes toward the elections emerged. The first was held by politically knowledgeable young people, interested in the elections and in public life, and possessing a constructively critical orientation toward the system. In this group, which I will call the *critical-knowledgeable* (or type 1), the genders were roughly equally represented. The second type comprised politically uninformed young people, all females. Aware of their deficiency, they were eager to repair it. Their social approach was integrationist, and they were keen on taking part in public life. This group is termed *integrationist-uninformed* (or type 2). The third group also consisted of uninformed informants, exclusively male, who attempted to hide their incompetence behind a mask of nonchalance or an oppositional stance to the political establishment. They were dubbed *oppositionary-uninformed* (or type 3). The size of the groups (seven males and seven females in type 1; nine females in type 2; and seven males in type 3) was accidental and is not discussed in this chapter.

Though the analytic role of the terms "profile," used in the first chapter, and "type" is analogous, I employ the second one here in order to differentiate between participant characteristics and content areas covered in the two chapters. As in chapter 1, here too, I first discuss the themes that emerge from the interviews and then present major findings in a table format that highlights general and type specific positions. The conclusions offer an in-depth analysis of political attitudes for the study group as a whole and for the three subgroups by type, exploring their significance for successful global citizenship.

IDENTITY: PERSONAL AND PUBLIC

Analysis of the young immigrants' social network highlights their attitudes toward personal versus civic identity and toward the upcoming elections. The informants had little exposure to civic activity typical of many local youths, partially because of a near-exclusive pool of same-culture friends. As shown in the previous chapter, males in particular were unwilling to socialize with local peers because they felt less powerful and did not want to establish informal intergroup relations on an unequal footing. Females described closer relations with local youth, especially in the context of cross-gender romantic ties. They were less threatened by asymmetrical intercultural connections and treated them as temporary. These differential attitudes substantiate mainstream contentions on power relations upheld by gender theorists (Bourdieu, 1990; Cameron, 1998; Romaine, 1999; Sunderland & Litosseliti, 2002).

All participants reported steering clear of political discussions, which were perceived as possible grounds for interpersonal conflicts. They avoided conversations with friends about the election, especially when differences of opinion were expected. Hess (2002) reports about similar patterns among American teenagers' discussions of controversial civic issues in secondary social studies classrooms and Glynn, Hayes, and Shanahan (1997) about adults' willingness to speak out in public debates as a function of perceived support versus opposition to the views they hold. Maxim explained: "I have my own Russian friends. With them, I talk about fun things to do, about everyday things, not elections!"

Unlike local youths, whose lives were less compartmentalized (Eisikovits & Karnieli, 1992), the immigrants made a clear distinction between personal and public domains. The cultural difference in attitudes to public affairs explains this discrepancy. Whereas native-born youngsters or long-time residents tended to be more civically disposed owing to membership in various voluntary youth organizations and movements (Kahane & Rapoport, 1990; Yogev & Shapira, 1990), their immigrant counterparts ascribed low importance to civic activity. Thus, arguments over elections had no place in their personal domain.

Even informants who were more politically knowledgeable (type 1) distinguished between their same-culture "friends" and host-culture "acquaintances." As in chapter 2, the term "friendship" was earmarked for Russian peers, and was never used to characterize relationships with local youths. Igor said: "Among pals I make no distinction: I have both *Olim* and *Sabras*. I have no expectations. If some day they betray me, it won't be a surprise. But from close friends I expect a lot." The issue of interpersonal trust and a generalized sense of vulnerability resurface here again. In each chapter further layers of meaning clarifying the importance of the same culture peer group are added, providing a fuller and deeper picture of their inner world.

Arkadi elaborated:

> It is easier to be friends with people who share your language. You choose friends according to their ability to understand you. If you mention a book or even a comic, it is enough to quote two words and everyone knows what you are talking about. Everything is different, not just the language. Body language, facial expressions mean different things to different people. A look is enough to understand what a friend means. For example, when *Sabras* talk fast I can't follow. Slang is particularly hard; when instant reactions are expected, it makes me feel like an idiot.

Despite their overwhelmingly Russian network of friends, the *critically-knowledgeable* informants maintained a firm civic identity. The dichotomy between private and public arenas explains why participants of this type did not perceive their social ties as interfering with their civic identification as Israelis.

Youths based their pre-election political attitude formation on various grounds. *Critical-knowledgeable* informants tended to emphasize independence in decision making, which can be interpreted as a reaction to the Soviet tradition of disregard for individualism. Vladimir clarified: "I am a reasonable person and I try to make rational decisions. I build my own interpretation of events rather than let the fact that I am an immigrant or young person affect my electoral choices."

By contrast, *integrationist-uninformed* participants regarded belonging to an immigrant family as the first identifier determining their attitudes to the elections. This corroborates Bronfenbrenner's contention about the Russian family atmosphere under the Communist regime that individual members superimposed the interest of the family unit on their own needs (Bronfenbrenner, 1970) which I had discussed in chapter 1. Pearson (1990) found the phenomenon, reinforced in this case by the all-female composition of the group, still characteristic for the post-*Perestroika* years. This trait has been largely adopted by Russian-Jewish immigrants. Members of the *oppositionary-uninformed* group referred to their collective identification as immigrants. They preferred this self-definition to the possibility of considering themselves Israelis. Alexis maintained: "When I go to the polling booth, I think of myself as an *Oleh* (new immigrant—singular), one who has nothing in common with the local people. This is the only way that feels comfortable to me."

Respondents of types 1 and 2 relied on both components of their identity—the immigrant and the Israeli—to formulate their position on voting, but differed in the weight they attributed to each component. The *critical-knowledgeable* youngsters, who were better informed about civic issues, gave the Israeli component more weight in their independent decision making, whereas the *integrationist-uninformed* group placed greater emphasis on their immigrant identity.

TWO POLITICAL WORLDS

Presidential elections in Russia happened to coincide with elections for Prime Minister and the *Knesset* (Israeli Parliament). Many respondents compared democracy in the new society with aspects of the Communist and present regimes in Russia. The issues they chose to highlight are indicative of the immigrants' overall attitude toward politics, politicians, and governance.

The *critical-knowledgeable* group delineated two aspects of the post-*Perestroika* regime in Russia. One was the impact of recent regime changes on people's everyday lives. Inna explained: "Now they have some kind of democracy. But there is anarchy and poverty. People don't have food to eat. They must care very little about the new democracy." The pragmatist orientation, I have already discussed, reemerges here. The lack of patience for ideologies succinctly formulated in Ilia's cynical comment in chapter 2 (p. 39) comparing between Communism and Zionism, highlights these youths' uniquely down-to-earth orientation, surprising for Western ears when coming from an 18-year-old. Apparently, growing up in a world where struggling for the basics of day-to-day existence is forefront, such preoccupations filter down to the young and shape their world views. The second issue on which they focused was the intimate connection between government and organized crime. Maxim elaborated:

> Politics in Russia is run by the Mafia nowadays. There is terrible corruption. Behind each member of Parliament you have a Mafia. They give you permission to buy and sell whatever you want from a ton of gold to a nuclear bomb. But you have to pay them the right percentage.

The dubious linkage between government and organized crime in this example is also directly relevant to individuals' sense of personal security – the threat of imminent danger brought about by the irresponsible trade in the most dangerous of weapons. Along similar lines, Nathan drew attention to another angle of government corruption during the earlier Soviet era further illuminating these participants' tradition of political skepticism:

> Elections in Russia were just a show. They claimed 97% voted when they knew that more than 50% didn't. In certain cities there weren't even any polling booths. How could they provide honest reports on voting percentages the same day for 290 million people without computers? It was just a show for the outside world.

Juxtaposition of the two political experiences provides insight into the way informants of type 1 formed their views on democracy. Igor clarified: "I appreciate the freedom that the democratic system here offers. People have so many choices. Maybe the local people don't see this, but I certainly do, because I know the difference from what we had there." Ellina cited a relativistic perspective, pointing out the predicament of citizens in a totalitarian regime who must fashion a survivalist strategy, foreign to those living in a world of rights and alternatives: "Democracy is more fun.

But when one has no alternative, one gets used to a different sort of regime, too. If you know you have to eat snow every morning, you do it." Perhaps the most developed perception of democracy was expressed by Nadia, who was able to go beyond concrete comparisons and offer an abstract conceptualization: "Democracy is good because it focuses on individuals as well as on society. It is simple psychology: where the individual is happy, society is satisfied."

Comparisons between "there" and "here" by the *integrationist-uninformed* respondents reflected their lack of civic orientation and skills. This was particularly clear in Olga's contention: "There we only had one party so we didn't have to think. Here there are so many possibilities. Who knows whether it's good or bad? All these differences cause tension among people. Having just one party would have solved many problems." This quote illustrates the cognitive and emotional distance these young women had to cover in their transition from one political culture to the other. Having to make choices was conceived as a particular hardship for persons who don't have this option as part of their mindset and for whom diversity was a source of insecurity. Such a statement is indicative of the extent of civic instruction necessary for meaningful participation in a democratic system.

Respondents from the all-female (type 2) group often applied collective language when distinguishing the two systems, a practice that reflected their insecurity (Brah, 1992; Hall, 1992; Maynard, 1994) and their need for a group identity to gain self-assurance. But they also voiced their eagerness to look ahead and learn about the new order. Natasha said: "Now we live here. We don't remember what went on there. Things changed. We don't fit in there any more."

By contrast, the *oppositionary-uninformed* wished to reinforce their connections with the old world and justify the continued relevance of those connections. This explains their self-imposed isolation in the present context. "Having lived there for so long, one is still curious about what is happening," said Michail. "I watch the preparations for elections in Russia on TV. There are six candidates for president; one of them is a millionaire. It's much more exciting." This group had no awareness of how politics in Israel affected them or how they could affect it. Members of this all-male group were cynical. They asserted their aspirations to a gender-appropriate position of power negatively by ridiculing the essence of democratic life and expressing disinterest in it. Sasha exclaimed: "Citizens' rights! It really sounds like something taken from a civics textbook or like party propaganda. It is nothing like what you see in real life."

As all informants and their families left behind an unsteady political structure, the transition to a new political culture, with its civic activities and elections, exerted a further disempowering effect (Horowitz, 1994). Common to all categories was an evaluative stance toward the political establishment in the host country, but with differing emphases. Members of the type 1 group based their position on information; those of type 2 on ignorance; while type 3 informants based it on scepticism.

SOURCES OF INFLUENCE

In political socialization research, youngsters are conventionally assumed to accept political messages without questioning them (Torney-Purta, 2000). As expected, in the style of political learning of Russian immigrant youths we found resistance to the transmitting political agents and their messages, particularly those representing the new society, such as schools and the media. In contrast, the family served as a repository of the country of origin, balancing the effect of these agents. The influence of peers was negligible.

The School

In their study of political socialization among nonimmigrant Israeli adolescents, Ichilov et al. (1989) assert that variables related to formal aspects of schooling (curriculum, instructional methods) exert only a minor influence on adolescents' political attitudes and behaviors. The open classroom climate, which provides opportunities for free self-expression and participation in a supportive environment, has a greater impact (Ichilov et al., 1989). The preferences of participants in the current study do not support this finding. Prioritizing the formal (as opposed to informal) aspects of schooling, as I have shown in the previous two chapters, they gave credit to the contribution of curricular content and teachers, whom they considered authority figures. This was particularly true for members of the *integrationist-uninformed* group. In her comparative study of the school's role in developing civic engagement in twenty-eight countries, Torney-Purta (2002) found that the formal curriculum, the culture of the classroom and the culture of the school are all important elements in civic education. However, for all three groups of informants in this study, classroom climate was far less relevant, as their intentions to participate in classroom debates were negligible.

Type 2 respondents more readily recognized school input in the formation of their political position. They perceived no threat to their stature in admitting that they possessed insufficient information for effective voting. Inna said: "School gave some basic knowledge about democracy, rights, and the electoral system." Nadia also appreciated the teachers' favorable influence: "Whatever I know about elections, I got from school.

Teachers expressed their views on politically significant issues without trying to impose them."

Most of the male informants, members of both the *critical-knowledgeable* and the *oppositionary-uninformed* groups, expected no assistance from school or from teachers, and regarded such assistance as degrading (Swan, 2002). Type 1 males thought it was the individual's job to develop their political standing by relying on personal resources and on the analysis of social and political processes. In line with the tendency demonstrated in chapters 1 and 2 these informants also wished to limit the role of the school to its academic functions. Type 3 youths, uncomfortable about admitting their incompetence (Swan, 2002), professed lack of interest in politics.

Ichilov (1991) also highlights the prevalence of gender-based differential schooling effects. More specifically, she indicates that schooling reinforces freedom of speech, involvement, and efficacy for males more than for females because of the fundamental male orientation of Western bureaucratic structures. Rosenthal, Rosenthal, and Jones (2001) report similar findings on gender based participation patterns in peer-group discussions. In contrast, in the present study schooling was found to be more empowering for young female immigrants.

Nevertheless, informants of both genders were loath to participate in classroom debates. As pointed out above, type 2 females conceded that their opinions were unformed, so they were embarrassed to participate. Type 3 males considered themselves "outsiders to the political game," as Misha noted. The *critical knowledgeable* felt that "discussions with classmates are childish," as Igor explained. He added: "I have my own position and I don't have the need to make myself heard. In other words, I don't care for an audience."

The Media

The media has been said to play a central role in political socialization (Chaffee, Nass, & Yang, 1990). While television is considered the most common vehicle for conveying relevant information to the young, supplementing it with newspaper and newsmagazine reading is deemed significant. Reliance on television alone is considered inadequate, leading to an unclear political orientation in adults (Chaffee et al., 1990; McLeod, 2000).

Along similar lines, Johansson (1991), who examined the relationship between the civic knowledge and values of Swedish adolescents and their mass-media exposure, concludes that the media (particularly television) should be viewed as one of many factors rather than an independent agent affecting the political culture of young people. However, Liebes and Ribak (1992) suggest, on the basis of their study of television influence on citizenship education of adolescents in Israel, that it does have a crucial impact on the development of political views. This is to be understood in light of the fact that over 75% of Israelis regularly watch the main evening news program. But their findings also establish a strong relationship between family culture and attitudes to freedom of the press and to the use of mediated information. In this sense, their conclusions cannot be attributed to the isolated impact of television but rather to the combined effect of family culture and media consumption.

Participants in the *critical-knowledgeable* group claimed to read newspapers regularly, specifically the political sections, to follow commentaries on the Internet, and to watch political discussions on television. The *integrationist-uninformed* respondents, mostly raised in families with lower educational levels, reported that TV was a major influence, but because parents watched mainly Russian channels and the family owned only one set, the youths could not gain broad access to political news. Several stated that just Russian-language (Israeli) newspapers were read in their homes, and that these were the only written media available to them. Peiser (2000) reports about an overall downward trend in newspaper reading among youth as a universal phenomenon. The *oppositionary-uninformed* group did not trust newspapers in any language and did not watch "propaganda" on television.

The Family

A study of the influence of family culture on political socialization of Israeli adolescents (Liebes & Ribak, 1992) found that the pluralist family, which allows children to provide meaningful input in family decision making, was more likely than autocratic families to induce political participation, owing to exposure to the media, political knowledge, and conversation (Ribak, 1997). Chaffee et al. (1990) further emphasized that youngsters whose parents encourage the expression of opinion in the home end up knowing more and being more active politically in school and in later life than those who are not provided opportunities for self-expression in their home environment. Neither contention is applicable to our study group, not even to type 1 youth who were raised by parents with academic degrees. Although political issues were discussed in their homes, these families did not provide a pluralist egalitarian atmosphere for their young members, as they typically lacked a tradition of intergenerational exchange of ideas, as I have shown in the first two chapters.

Dolan (1995) investigated the impact of an intact versus a single-parent family household structure on the political efficacy of the young people in it. The assumption that youngsters experienced different political socialization in the two types of household was not substantiated. No relationship was found between political efficacy, knowledge or participation and family structure. However, in the present study, which included several informants raised in single-parent families, the interviews revealed that these spent less time discussing politics because of economic constraints that led to more intensive work involvement by the single parents.

Critical-knowledgeable informants perceived the family as the entity in which their original Russian cultural identity was preserved. This was crucial to them despite their civic interest in the new political scene. Yet, although they were aware of their parents' positions on elections and identified the family as the main context for the development of political attitudes, they claimed self-determination in their ultimate electoral choices. "My parents care only about security. I listen to what they have to say because they have more experience, but eventually I make my own decisions," said Vladimir.

Ellina, of type 1, wagered that "in all houses people must be talking about the elections now." But this was a false impression. Despite their intense identification with family interests, members of type 2 could only guess their parents' positions, as these were not debated. This was due either to overexertion (as Marina said, "Everybody is so busy we hardly see each other. We have little time to talk about these things") or to an absence of information and a habit of family discussions.

To foster their rebel-like self-portrayal, participants of type 2 claimed to be unaware of their parents' political views and professed to be indifferent to them. Sasha left no room for misunderstanding: "Why should I care about my family's opinions on the elections? Personally, I don't give a damn about politics, so why vote? This stuff means nothing to me."

The similarity between types 2 and 3 in the absence of family discussions notwithstanding, their positions on this state of affairs differed. While the *integrationist-uninformed* group saw this absence as regrettable, the *oppositionary-uninformed* took a nonchalant approach, as part of the detached image they wished to project.

Peers

The influence of peers on political socialization has not received much attention in the literature. When mentioned, their influence is usually compared with that of the family and is found to be less powerful (Tedin,

1980). This was corroborated by the findings of the present study. As we have shown, the informants claimed to have refrained from discussing political views with same-culture peers, whereas their contact with host-culture peers was reported as limited.

The literature emphasizes peer influence usually in the context of involvement in youth organizations (Yogev & Shapira, 1990; Kahane & Rapoport, 1990). Because our respondents did not participate in informal educational frameworks, the potential of such frameworks to serve as political socializing agents was practically nonexistent. The absence of this experience from their lives placed them at a disadvantage relative to host-culture peers in opportunities for constructing democratic attitudes and reduced their political proficiency.

UTILIZING POTENTIAL OUTCOMES OF ELECTIONS

The interest youths manifest in politics and their readiness for civic participation are affected by their attitudes toward the system of governance. Because of their low level of political expertise, interviewees of types 2 and 3 could not envisage ways of utilizing the potential outcomes of the elections optimally. Even the *critical-knowledgeable* group found it difficult to define such changes. "I have a problem with this. I can't see the future," explained Slava. They were unimaginative when given full rein to suggest desirable lines of action. This was also found to be the case with young Americans and long-time Israeli residents (Eisikovits, Hedin, & Adam, 1984).

Type 1 participants were against narrow ethnic parties and, because of their broader identification with the new society, supported large parties with more comprehensive aims.[2] Their positions were well phrased and grounded. Vladimir said: "I am against sectoral lists and votes. We won't get far if we divide into groups according to ethnic criteria." Nadia stated: "A party of new immigrants based on narrow interests is not viable. It does not present a real program for action. You don't even know whether it's right or left wing. Pure nonsense!"

In contrast, most of the *integrationist-uninformed* group were dedicated to immigrant issues and were convinced that the immigrants' party could cater best to their needs. Claudia asserted: "What is important is to attain more support for *Olim*, cheaper apartments, more jobs. I don't know which party to vote for, which will be best for me."

For the *oppositionary-uninformed* group, disbelief in the system justified indifference to politics. They presented their dearth of civic knowledge as a matter of choice, indeed, as an ideology of resistance. In effect, because of the self-imposed marginality and limited substantive knowledge of type

3 informants, their ability to use elections as a medium for change was minimal.

For all three groups, the political legacy brought from their country of origin did not encourage informants to develop civic competence. Ex-Soviet citizens tended to consider themselves subjects of changes imposed from above rather than change agents able to have an impact on their sociopolitical environment (Gitelman, 1995; Zilberg & Leshem, 1996). The tentativeness of the young informants' answers concerning their wishes for election-induced reforms suggests that they saw little chance of bringing about change. Although they paid lip service to the advantages of democracy, because of their generalized distrust of governance, they saw the distinction between totalitarianism and democracy primarily as a difference in rhetoric.

Table 3.1 summarizes the informants' perspectives on voting and politics.

CONCLUDING COMMENTS

In the personal history of participants in this study, civic identity carried negative associations. In the former Soviet context, it connoted exclusion for belonging to a Jewish minority, despite the professed ideology of egalitarianism which denied differentiation on ethnic grounds. Knowledge about the Soviet system was acquired through cross-generational transmission rather than from personal experience. These negative associations metamorphosed into an instrumental approach to officialdom at large. As a result, elections in Israel came to be regarded—more blatantly for types 2 and 3—as a vehicle for achieving direct gains (e.g., more support for immigrants, cheaper apartments) rather than as a rite of passage to adulthood. Because they were not involved in grassroots politics, the immigrant youths tended to overestimate the value of voting as a means of civic self-expression; for them, it was virtually the only vehicle of public participation.

Notwithstanding the differences in political ethos between Russia and Israel, there were several similarities between these young immigrants and their local counterparts, as shown by a comparison between the current study and Ichilov et al.'s (1989) research. Informants from families with only a rudimentary education (mainly type 2) were apt to apply democratic precepts in a way similar to that of native-born or veteran youths from the lower sociodemographic strata. Youths from educated families (mostly classified as type 1) relied on their parents, as did advantaged veteran youth from higher socioeconomic backgrounds. These participants

Table 3.1. Perspectives on Voting and Politics

Theme	General	Critical Knowledgeable	Integrationist Uninformed (All Female Group)	Oppositionary Uninformed (All Male Group)
Identity: Personal and public	- Made clear distinction between personal and public domains of life. - Had a near-exclusive pool of same-culture friends. - Ascribed low importance to civic activity, and therefore arguments over elections had no place in their personal domain (same-culture peer activity).	- Despite their network of overwhelmingly Russian friendships, they held a firm civic identity. - Emphasized independence in decision making about electoral choices.	- Civic identification was not crystallized. - Saw belonging to an immigrant family the first identifier determining their attitudes toward the elections.	- Claimed to be uninterested in inter-cultural ties with Israelis or in civic activity. - Referred to their collective identification as immigrants for determining their attitudes toward the elections.
Two political worlds	- Compared perspectives on democracy in the new society with aspects of communist and present regimes in Russia.	- Valued the democratic system highly.	- Were eager to look ahead and learn about the new order.	- Cynical and negative: they ridiculed the essence of democratic life and expressed disinterest in it.

- An evaluative stance toward the political establishment in the receiving country was common to all categories, but with differing emphases.	- Based their position on information.	- Based their position or [the absence of a position] on ignorance.	- Based their position on scepticism.

Sources of Influence

The School

- Expected no assistance from school or from teachers. Regarded such assistance as degrading. Thought it was the individual's job to develop a political standing through reliance on personal resources and analysis of social and political processes.	- Gave credit to the contribution of curricular content and of teachers to their political socialization. Females more readily recognized school input in the formation of their political position. They were not embarrassed to admit they had insufficient information for effective voting. Schooling was more empowering for female students.	- Expected no assistance from school or teachers. Uncomfortable about admitting their incompetence, professed lack of interest in politics.

Table continues on next page.

Table 3.1. Continued

Theme	General	Critical Knowledgeable	Integrationist Uninformed (All Female Group)	Oppositionary Uninformed (All Male Group)
The Media		- Read newspapers regularly, specifically the political sections; watched political discussions and commentaries on television.	- TV was a major influence. Watched Russian channels and read Russian newspapers, if at all, because those were the only sources available in the home.	- Did not trust newspapers in any language and did not watch "propaganda" on TV.
The Family	- Families did not provide a pluralist egalitarian atmosphere for their young members, as they typically lacked a tradition of intergenerational exchange of ideas.	- Although they were aware of their parents' positions on elections and identified the family as the main context for the development of political attitudes, they claimed self-determination in their ultimate electoral choices.	- Despite their intense identification with family interests, respondents could only guess their parents' positions, as these were not debated. The family had a limited impact on their choices.	- To foster their rebel-like self-portrayal, they claimed to be unaware of their parents' political views and professed to be indifferent to them.

Peers	- Peer influence usually occurs in the context of involvement in youth organizations. The absence of this experience placed respondents at a disadvantage compared with host-culture peers regarding opportunities for constructing democratic attitudes.	
Utilizing potential outcomes of elections	- The political legacy brought from their country of origin did not encourage the development of civic competence. The tentativeness of their answers concerning wishes for election-induced reforms suggests that they saw little chance of bringing about change. - Though knowledgeable, they were unimaginative when given the opportunity to suggest desirable lines of action.	- Because of lack of expertise, could not envisage ways of utilizing the potential outcomes of the elections optimally.

Table continues on next page.

Table 3.1. Continued

Theme	General	Critica Knowledgeable	Integrationist Uninformed (All Female Group)	Oppositionary Uninformed (All Male Group)
		- Against narrow ethnic parties. Because of their broader identification with the new society, they supported large parties with more varied aims.	- In contrast to type 1, were dedicated to immigrant issues or were convinced that the immigrants' party could cater best to their needs.	- Because of their self-imposed marginality and limited substantive knowledge, their ability to use elections as a medium for change was limited.

were similarly more exposed to the print media, which provided detailed information and an analytical perspective on civic issues.

The *critical-knowledgeable* informants and most of the *integrationist-uninformed* youngsters (i.e., more than two thirds of the respondents) held democracy in high esteem when compared with Soviet socialism. In contrast, the *oppositionary-uninformed* (all seven) and a few type 2 interviewees (three) saw advantages in the prescriptive pre-*Perestroika* era.

Type 1 interviewees felt capable of influencing society through elections. Consistent with the comparative study of Israeli and American young people's attitudes toward voting (Eisikovits, Hedin, & Adam, 1984), they believed that their votes counted. These youths identified with the broad interests of the state and considered themselves ready for participation, although they had no specific suggestions to offer for alternative sociopolitical scenarios.

Interviewees of type 2 (all-females) also found elections crucial. Because they viewed themselves as less adept in this area, they spoke with insecurity stemming from a vulnerable self-perception in public matters as members of a double minority. The *oppositionary-uninformed* adopted a transnational identity, with their cultural orientation turned to the past. These informants, although doubtful about the impact of their votes, were determined to use them to advance immigrant concerns.

Type 2 and type 3 participants were largely confined to supporting the special-interest immigrant party, owing to their limited public knowledge base. This further deepened their social isolation and avoidance of civic involvement. Lack of experience in decision making at the school, youth organization, or community level—parameters that were found to induce a positive disposition toward voting among veteran Israeli and American youths—fostered a passive self-image among the *integrationist-uninformed* and the *oppositionary-uninformed* respondents.

All three types were handicapped by the attitudes to politics they had brought along from their country of origin. Reticence to engage in political discussion, which they classified as a method characteristic of the former Soviet totalitarian regime, impeded their civic engagement and development in the country of migration.

While local youths considered classroom discussions or debates during activities of various youth movements as occasions for opinion formation and potential sources for the enrichment of their political knowledge, these immigrant youths identified such encounters as possible traps liable to lead to ideological coercion. The *critical knowledgeable* used individualism as a safety valve against outside "intrusion." In other words, first-source and parent-transmitted memories from their country of emigration overshadowed the civic experiences of these youths in their receiving society.

Political science research documents a decline in the youth's public knowledge and participation in Western democracies, and the situation among immigrant youths in transition between political cultures can be expected to be only worse. McLeod (2000) claims that although youth voting in the United States is low, community based civic engagement is flourishing. Our study portrays a reverse relationship between these two types of activities among Russian immigrant youths. Voting, described by Dudley and Gitelson (2002) as the lowest level of public engagement, is the only form of political action they recognize and practice. But even this minimal participation is in jeopardy because of the youths' lack of civic skills. Their risk of losing faith in voting is increasing due to their unrealistic expectations from elections.

This can be a dangerous trend, understudied in research about the political engagement of young people. It calls attention to the unique patterns of political participation of immigrant youths, and thus to the importance of studying them in their broader cultural context. Unlike the fast rate of Americanization noted by Stepick and Stepick (2002) among immigrant youths in the United States, our study group exhibited lasting attachment to core values of their culture of origin. Moreover, the strong effect of the political tradition of the country of emigration is illustrated by all subgroups in this study.

Immigrant youths constitute a proliferating sector in voting populations worldwide. They make up the most sizeable source of population growth in Western democracies, and their impact on the political future of these regimes is undeniable. In his essay on educating for democratic behavior in an intercultural context, Lanir (1991) makes a distinction among "democratic knowing", "democratic thinking" and "democratic doing" relevant for this study. The alienation and political incompetence displayed by members of two out of the three types described in this paper, and the overall lack of experience in "democratic doing" of all three types may prove costly for democratic regimes. Systematic study of the interplaying variables affecting views and attitudes of young immigrants from various countries, of the kind undertaken in this study, may help receiving societies enhance the civic literacy and efficient political engagement of their immigrant youths.

This study demonstrates that students' perceptions of government are bound up with their personal, communal, ethnic, and national experiences. Their conception of history shapes what they can and do learn in classrooms. Therefore, special efforts must be invested in providing immigrant students with opportunities for gaining increased civic proficiency in their receiving society. Intervention efforts, including both formal and informal components, must follow a thorough investigation of the political tradition of the country of origin.

Civic literacy and involvement are particularly important at a time when globalization is in the process of changing political orders and power balances (Sassen, 1996). In such times lack of political know-how and interest are dangerous for the individual and undercut his/her ability to act for a just and enjoyable world to live in. Hence, immigrant youths should be skilled and willing to put their hands deep into the pot of global governance because novel forms of belonging open up for them through such means as absentee voting and multiple citizenship. Paradigmatic changes in the conception of the nation state, facing challenges from supernational economic forces and alignments, open up new opportunities along with new risks. It takes engaged, critical participation to make the first ones prevail.

NOTES

1. A group of graduate students—S. Cohen, O. Eshbal, Y. Herzog, H. Kuperman, S. Ofir, H. Schechter, and E. Steinfeld—who participated in a research seminar titled "Education in a Multicultural Society" which I offered, helped with the data collection. I am solely responsible for data analysis and write-up of the study.
2. Among the 11 parties elected to the 120-seat *Knesset*, there were several ethnically based lists. One of them, *Israel B'Aliyah* catered specifically to the needs of Russian immigrants and received seven seats.

CHAPTER 4

"THERE (IN THE SERVICE) YOU WILL HAVE TO BECOME PART OF THINGS"

Acculturation in and through the Military

The cross-cultural transition and social integration of immigrant youths and young adults constitute pivotal problems in immigrant receiving societies, as these immigrants are considered a population at risk. Not only are they undergoing the drastic change of immigration, but they are also in the midst of their identity formation and face a myriad of decisions regarding future life goals which carry the risk of failure and of sliding into delinquency, drug abuse, and antisocial behavior. Though integrative opportunities for individuals are available in institutions of higher education and work places, most societies do not offer universalistic structures for social and cultural adjustment to the post high-school age group. However, in Israel, compulsory military service does, according to popular belief, provide an acculturative framework for these young people. A thorough search of the relevant literature yielded no systematic sources dealing with immigrant soldiers in countries other than Israel. Thus, a 10-year scan of titles and abstracts of the international journal *Armed Forces and Society*, one of the mainstream periodicals in this domain,

Immigrant Youth Who Excel: Globalization's Uncelebrated Heroes, pp. 77–94
Copyright © 2008 by Information Age Publishing

revealed no results. Consequently, no comparative information on the mutual relationship between military service and young immigrants is available. A question that arises, but is beyond the scope of this book, is whether in other countries alternative institutions fulfill some of the functions of the compulsory military service in Israel.

This study examines how a group of immigrant youths from the large urban centers of the European republics of the Former Soviet Union (FSU) who arrived during the 1990s, the research population for this whole series of studies, experienced their army service and how the military affected their sociocultural adaptation. In the previous three chapters I focused on the academic adjustment of 17–18-year-olds from the same background to the Israeli school system and their comparative evaluation of educational experiences in the two countries, as well as on gender differences in the cross-cultural adaptation styles of these youths. These studies indicated, I would like to remind the reader, that participants distinguished between short- and long-range social and educational goals and opted for gradual integration on terms they themselves negotiated. These youths, particularly males, rejected integrative efforts initiated by the schools as artificial. They thought that rapprochement between immigrant and veteran youths would be best served by immersion in total life situations, such as those provided by the draft. Contrasting the school and the service, Igor, one of the participants quoted in chapter 2 (p. 38) claimed: "There [in the army] you will have to become part of things. You can't run home to your parents and friends. Also, when people's lives depend on each other, that draws them together automatically." The present study investigates the mode and extent to which these expectations have been fulfilled.

The military has been looked upon as a major factor in Israel's nation-building effort since independence in 1948 (Ben-Shalom & Horenczyk, 2004; Carmeli & Fadlon, 1997; Shield, 1973). This is so since it brings together youth from all walks of life for an intensive period of service.[1] Contrary to this widely accepted proposition, Azarya and Kimmerling (1983) contend that identifying the Israel Defense Forces (IDF) as a people's army is a myth. They claim that the army never invested effort to include immigrants into its core, but rather allocated them to the margins, thereby underscoring their peripheral position. Though the service helped them become members of the larger community, it did not facilitate their progression towards the center of society.

By the early 90s (10 years after the Azarya and Kimmerling (1983) study), the IDF had undergone a transformation in the overall perception of its role, becoming a smaller, more professional organization (Cohen, 1997). In this process it divested some of its allocated public functions, particularly those related to serving as a vehicle for social integration and an equalizer of opportunities. Yet, the popular image of the people's army has persisted, outliving the above change in orientation. It is worth mentioning that in few countries is civic inclusion of immigrants in matters civic considered such a high priority. Even the state auditor, the highest level investigative official appointed by Parliament to oversee the activities and budgetary actions of various ministries, expected it to act according to these principles. In a special section in the 1999 yearly report, the auditor's office found the performance of the Israeli army deficient in terms of maximizing the potential of new immigrant soldiers.

This gap between the growing professionalization of the army and its perception as a social integrator provides a confusing double message to military age young immigrants from the FSU. Owing to family hardships, financial difficulties, and language problems, these immigrant draftees are sorely in need of supportive services. For these same reasons, many of them wish to serve close to their homes, which makes them unfit for combat units; thus, they tend to be relegated to administrative or auxiliary units that are already overpopulated and in least need of manpower. Hence, immigrant draftees are more likely to be released from duty based on economic grounds.[2] Within the context of how army experience affects immigrant acculturation, the current study thus also considers the impact of this situation upon our immigrant respondents.

THE STUDY

The research took place one year following the completion of military service, at a time when participants were enrolled as students in various institutions of higher education. These participants have been selected because they were believed to have high chances to adjust given their intellectual abilities. They were assumed to possess good verbal skills which would enable them to provide vivid reports about their service. This is a phenomenological study seeking to gain an understanding of the subjective meaning of experiences for the persons who took part in them and are able to provide comprehensive descriptions of these experiences (Moustakas, 1994). From these individual descriptions I derived basic structural patterns characteristic of the phenomena studied. The focus is on in-depth subjective analysis of personal experiences rather than on generalizations. However, such an analysis at the same time provides solid exploratory ground for heuristic model building upon which studies aimed at rigorous generalizations can be based (Babbie, 2004). This timing was chosen due to logistic difficulties involved in conducting research with active soldiers, as well as to allow time for the formation of a reflective perspective. The study was based on semistructured retrospective individual interviews with 16 young men and the same number of young women.[3] It should be noted that most participants had spent at least 5 years in their new country at the time of this research. The men were 22 and the women 21 years old.

The retrospective interview guide followed a chronological order and focused on three consecutive time periods: preceding the draft, during the service and the postservice phase. The hazards of retrospective interviewing notwithstanding (Bertaux, 1981; Bourdieu, 1986; Flick, 2006), interviewees attempted to recall their impressions and feelings by visualizing and recounting specific events, which helped them remember their context.

Most participants enjoyed the interview situation, regarding it as an opportunity to reflect on the service and discuss it with Israelis who were knowledgeable about these milieux. The interviews took place at a time and place chosen by the informants and were characterized by a pleasant cooperative atmosphere.

Following the lines of the interview, results are presented in three different time periods: attitudes prior to being drafted, experiences during army service and impact upon their current lives. In each stage, immigrant experiences and attitudes (and those of their parents) are often juxtaposed with the contrasting behavior of veteran Israeli draftees and their families, so as to underscore the unique characteristics of the research group.

Before the Draft: Attitudes to the Service

The interviewees' attitudes toward enlistment were influenced by several factors, which often combined to operate as serious deterrents to serving in the army. One of the main influences in this respect was their parents. The participants, who grew up in an adult-dominated world, often presented their opinions as a reflection of their parents' ideas, possibly because they believed it added authority to their claims. In fact, it was almost impossible to separate the voices of the recruits from the echoed views of their parents—a feature that can be attributed to the enmeshed character of Russian Jewish families. Parental influence is a central and recurring motif. Its impact on these young adults, that I am dwelling upon throughout this volume, is particularly interesting in view of my demonstrated contention regarding their psychological and often physical absence from their teenage children's social integration in the country of migration. The effect of enmeshment must have been almighty to persist under these circumstances.

The parents tended to hold a negative view of bureaucracy in general and the military in particular, owing to their pragmatist instrumentalist approach to officialdom. In chapters 1 and 2 we have seen that this approach has been apparently bequeathed to the young generation, as we have heard very similar views expressed by two successful profile I male informants, Sergey in chapter 1 and Oleg in chapter 2 concerning the expected role of the school, the representative of officialdom in their day-to-day existence. Dima, the only officer in the group, offered the following insight:

> In Russia, whoever managed to avoid the army was seen as macho. So my parents wanted me to continue my studies. For them, the military was a waste of time. Their friends treated the news about my becoming an officer as a bad joke. "Officers' training?! Why would he need that nonsense?"

Seen as a public service, parents perceived the Israeli army as useless for the individual. That is, the civic and the individual were perceived as separate incompatible realms.

These attitudes were reinforced by stories and myths about the Soviet army and its horrors, which was the store of military knowledge harbored in the family.

Misha explained:

> We brought this view of the army from Russia. There, only crazy people wanted to be drafted, but you went to prison if you refused. Prison there is no fun. So motivation for the draft here was nonexistent. I simply wanted to get it over with. Had it not been compulsory, they would never have seen me.

Extrapolation from the previous sphere of experience is direct. There is no attempt to give present experience a new chance. In the mindset of *homo sovieticus* (Horowitz, 1989), young as old, thoroughly disenchanted from life in a totalitarian regime, participation in civic matters is naturally identified as coercion. Misha had no qualms about voicing uncomplimentary views, regardless of the high status of the service among veteran Israelis, of which he was aware.

As if to complete this negative influence, rather than counterbalance it, the interviews revealed a dearth of knowledge about the Israeli army, and how it contrasted with its Soviet counterpart. For its part, the IDF, which was becoming more professional and hence not interested in expanding recruitment, invested little in information dissemination. The first to be hurt under these circumstances are underinformed groups, such as immigrants and young people from the lower socioeconomic echelons who lack personal sources of information.

While among Israelis the service is discussed in patriotic terms (Cohen, 1997), members of the research group viewed it as nothing but an obligation and thus had low personal expectations. Under this premise, the use of expressions such as "planning the years of service" or "choosing a task," which are in common use among local conscripts, was inconceivable for this group. Oleg elaborated: "I knew nothing about what's ahead. I heard about the army from television and from students in my class, but I had no personal knowledge. So I could not make any plans."

Lack of information worked hand in hand with negative attitudes to the military. Immigrant parents, as perceived by members of the study group, felt a double sense of powerlessness. First, as newcomers who were not knowledgeable about the system, they did not see how they could influence the course of their offspring's service in any way. Second, as bearers of the image of the Soviet army as the worst symbol of despotic power, these parents did not believe that any individual could exercise acts of free will within such an institution. Boris explained: "My parents knew very little about army stuff. When I was pleased, they were pleased, too. They felt unable to change things anyway. People from Russia are used to such feelings." Nina also said: "My parents didn't think girls' service should be compulsory. It was against their values and mentality. Did it help?!"[4]

This lack of parental engagement was particularly conspicuous because of its contrast to the position common among Israeli parents, who are highly involved in their youngsters' service-related problems (Cohen, 1997). Local parents see the army as an opportunity for their children's personal development, as do the youngsters themselves, who look forward to their service as a chance to enhance individuation and allow them identification with national values (Lieblich & Perlow, 1988). Parents often advocate for their children's rights when these seem jeopardized, and help them with their choice of military jobs using multigenerational army knowledge, personal contacts and accumulated expertise (Cohen, 1995). Through this support, the nonimmigrant recruits manage to maintain an active stance, seeking personal fulfillment in their roles. Indeed, parental involvement in service conditions has become so great, often resulting in the exposure of the army to media criticism, that it has come to be regarded as a growing problem among military circles, as it threatens to interfere with the conduct of day-to-day work in the ranks (Cohen, 1997).

According to our informants, their parents concentrated on personal and family implications of the service, supported minimalist input, and advised their children to adopt a similar attitude. Parents guided their sons and daughters to prefer personal safety and logistic considerations (such as proximity to home) in decisions about army placements, rather than using substantive grounds, like concern for the job itself. Arkadi, for example, was interested in computers and would have liked to do something related to this field in the army. However, his family opposed such a move, as it would have meant being stationed farther away from home. He complied: "They were worried about me, so I became a food supplier for eighteen bases in the northern region, traveling, like a robot, on the same roads all the time. At home at night I worked on my computer." He bowed to these constraints, caught between parental injunctions and army regulations.

Several respondents indicated that they were unable to translate their army stories to Russian for their parents. These were Israeli experiences, which their parents did not share. Symbolically, they lacked the common language to discuss them. Whereas in immigrant families, the world over, the young are often the heralds of change, bringing in new knowledge gained from their various channels of communication with the outside world, with which they frequently have more contact than their elders, in this case this route for innovation is barred. In any case, the military did not constitute a topic of conversation, as the parents were disinterested in the youngsters' army jobs and experiences. They categorized the latter as public service, which only existed to oppress the individual.

In Israeli households, in contrast, army experiences are a central topic of conversation during soldiers' home visits, serving as an intergenerational bridge. The rapprochement between the public and private domains, due to long-standing army camaraderie, is a typical characteristic of Israeli society (Helman, 1999), as is a basic feeling of identification with the army and recognition of its role as a protector of personal security in a nation under constant security tension (Azaryahu, 1999; Ben-Yehuda, 1999).

DURING THE SERVICE: THE MILITARY EXPERIENCE

In considering the army experiences of the research group (men and women alike), we borrow Lieblich and Perlow's typology (1988) of male soldiers:

1. "from fear to mastery"—those who entered with fear and low expectations of their own performance, but succeeded in coping with hardships and ended up with a positive summary of their conscription;
2. "weathering the storm"—those who entered with low expectations and barely managed to make it through the service, thus evaluating it negatively;

3. "disappointments"—those who started out with high hopes but ended up frustrated with their service, due to a series of unpleasant experiences;

4. "hopes fulfilled"—those who entered with positive expectations and succeeded in fulfilling them.

Applying this typology to our study group, several of the male informants' experiences fit the "weathering the storm" and "disappointments" categories. Unfamiliar with the system, they felt incapable of negotiating for change of placement when dissatisfied with their jobs. As Alex noted: "I had no idea about other jobs. Why should they prefer me over someone else at another unit? Besides, how would I find my way through all this bureaucracy? It's too much trouble." Due to inaction, many passed up chances for improving the quality of their service and preferred to stick it out in their original position. Consistent with findings in chapter two regarding the marginalizing effect of ethnic-enclosure and lack of willingness to adjust, particularly among male informants, we are confronted here with the penalizing outcomes of this stance.

As a result, advancement and change of jobs often only occurred through the intervention or recommendation of their commanders. As Koba indicated: "I was sent to all kinds of courses. I didn't say 'I am the best, why don't you send me?' They chose me. I certainly didn't push myself. I enjoyed everything I learned there." Many new immigrant soldiers even turned down summonses to officers' courses, which would have been considered signs of special distinction by native or veteran soldiers. Although they attempted to dichotomize the public and the private, the two spheres are actually shown to nourish each other (see pp. 82–84). Thus missing opportunities in the former implies losing chances for personal gains in the latter.

This push for advancement by their commanding officers may reflect a social awareness approach that competes with the new trend towards professionalism in the army. Apparently, professionalization is internalized at a differential rate by various members of this vast, complex organization. Officers and trainers who have been socialized according to the social awareness approach do not divest it instantaneously. So these immigrant soldiers also encountered officers who functioned in line with the integrative model. The occasional coexistence of the two approaches in certain units confused these recruits. Decreased representation of "integrationist" commanders is bound to result in a cutback in these conscripts' channels for advancement.

Gender based difference in behavioral patterns seems as conspicuous here as in the previous chapter. Although the army in Israel, the US. and elsewhere is generally portrayed as a man's world (Ben-Ari, 1998;

O'Dunivin, 1994), female voices in this study were louder and clearer when describing their experiences in the service. Anna reflected: "I did not expect to be given such responsibility. My commanding officer trusted my decisions even though my Hebrew was not perfect." Satisfaction with their jobs placed most female participants in the positive categories "from fear to mastery" and "hopes fulfilled."

Female soldiers, whose job options were more restricted, were impressed with the authority bestowed upon them in their clerical positions. This job satisfaction contributed to their overall satisfaction with their service. They were flattered to represent the system. As Marina said: "Only a few months ago I was standing in line filling out forms and asking for assistance as a new immigrant. Now I was sitting behind the desk helping others."

Regardless of gender, those who moved "from fear to mastery" and those with "hopes fulfilled" relished in the responsibility placed upon them and regarded the military as an integrative body. In contrast, those who were "weathering the storm" or who suffered "disappointments" felt that they were placed at a disadvantage. Michail contended: "I thought the military would make me feel like a real Israeli. Looking back, I realize I had fewer chances, less options to choose from than the *Sabras*." The dissatisfied opted for marginality, with the motto: "I want to be my own boss." Vladi, for example, chose to be a cook after having been refused a job in electronics, his area of interest. He explained:

> It's a long story why I became a cook. But this is where I was accepted [he said ironically]. I got used to it. I was my own master. Didn't have to mind anybody. I would go down to the kitchen and spend all day there.

In his case, independence served as a substitute for meaningfulness on the job.

On the overt level, there was no expectation that the army should fulfill individual wishes; as a civic service, it was not expected to be of personal use. Nonetheless, members of both genders appeared to have internalized the orientations of local youths in evaluating the military, as a whole, according to satisfaction with their jobs. As Masha, voicing her own experience, stated: "You know, each morning when I came into the office, the people there made me feel that what I do makes a difference." In a less positive vein, Sasha said: "Some of my friends learned useful stuff in the army, stuff they can even use outside. They at least got something for their time."

In short, the actual military experience itself varied for our study group. The women seem to have been more satisfied with their positions and hence with their service, while the men were more likely to view this period of their lives as something to be withstood.

POSTSERVICE PHASE: AFTER EFFECTS

Only a few informants developed a reflective approach about their service. The year that had gone by since their release had not been used for the formation of a critical perspective on the army experience. Viewing the civic and the individual as incompatible realms, many shared the opinion that, since the military is compulsory, it should not be expected to impact upon one's personal life. This can be seen in a wide range of issues related to their current lives.

Army Friendships

The rich tradition of army friendships is a main feature of Israeli society, one that brings the military (as part of the public sector) closer together with the individual lives of soldiers, thereby turning the IDF into an integral part of civilian life in Israel (Helman, 1999). These durable ties become networks of mutual help in civilian life, and members make it a chief concern to stay in the same reserve units for years.[5]

Among these immigrant soldiers, however, the few friendships that survived the service were with same-culture peers—particularly for the males. These relationships were able to withstand the test of time because of the common cultural background rather than the shared military experience.[6] Nikolai remarked: "I had a few Russian and a few Israeli friends, but most friendships, particularly those with Israelis, didn't last because we all went back to our own lives." This is in line with their preference to see the army service as a period with a clear end, rather than include the soldier identity into their ongoing life circumstances and membership as reservists. Such discontinuity becomes all the more conspicuous in light of the close connections with Israelis that some maintained during the army. In Lev's words: "We would go out to eat together, to pubs, visited each other's homes, were invited to one another's family events, and so on." Nevertheless, these ties were severed.

Females in particular were favorably surprised by the good relationships they established with Israeli peers in the army, in light of preconceived notions that they communicated to each other about Israeli attitudes towards the "Russians." As Genia claimed: "I never thought we could get so close. I always figured we were so different we'd never find a common language." This expectation may be the result of unpleasant social experiences in school. According to Sveta: "In class, we were only five immigrant girls, so they ignored us. I wouldn't even dream that the military could be a time of fun and friendship with Israelis." Yet, although girls portrayed the integrative role of the army as more important, they too reported negatively about maintaining the friendships formed there. As Lara admitted: "It has been my fault because I don't return calls, I am too busy."

Thus, at the end of their service, most interviewees of both genders decided to return to their secluded premilitary world. This was despite the females' efforts to pass for Israelis in their appearance, as Clarina pointed out: "I just didn't want to look different from everybody, that's all." Boris summed up his army ties with host culture peers in the following way: "We had a good time and common issues while in the military. But that's where it ended." This clear division between military and civil life emphasizes these immigrant respondents' fear and suspicions of the wider Israeli society and their preference for the security of the closed, in-group world. In this mindset the military was considered an imposed break, or, at best, a moratorium. In other words, no aspect of the service is defined as personal. In order to make this separation, they prefer to cut all ties created during their service by including them in the large category of the army-as-public experience.

Civic Identity

Attitudes to civic identity varied greatly, with a wider representation of voices that preferred seclusion from the greater society to those favoring integration. There were those who, like Sergey, claimed: "You have to be born here [in Israel] to belong. I don't even try to become what I can't and the service didn't change that."

Along with this deterministic attitude were voices, like those of Vadim, which distinguished between civic and social identity: "A citizen, yes. But the year in the service did not change my mentality. I don't think I'll ever be an Israeli." Ania also identified social integration with personal change: "I want to fit in, but that doesn't mean I will leave my values behind. My world view is set. In the army I had to get along with Israelis, so I am more tolerant of other people's behavior now. But I was sixteen when I came here. That's too late to change."

Olga advanced yet another position. Disregarding culturally based distinctions, she stated: "Everyone who lives in Israel is an Israeli. I have my past, which is in the Ukraine, and my present, which is in Israel. I don't mix them up and they don't disturb each other. The service was no exception to this rule." She accepted the fact that her life was and will remain compartmentalized, claiming no need to put the pieces together. Fear of change is a recurrent motif which masks the deeper angst concerning loss of identity. However, accepting fragmentation of identity as a natural state of being, is, in fact, a sign of globalized existence (Basok, 2002; Bauman, 1998).

Finally, expressing an integrationist view, Koba used a striking metaphor: "In the army I got to know Israelis personally, so the country was no longer this indecipherable beast. Instead, I became part of it." The "indecipherable beast" encapsulates it all: lack of trust imported from previous existence, dread of strangers and hesitance to open up.

Similar to their attitudes to old army friends, the vast majority of informants seem to support differentiation from Israeli civic society, tending to invest little in attempts at acculturation. This lack of effort can be attributed to feelings of alienation and negative predispositions, reinforced by the mixed messages disseminated by the military establishment.

Acquired Skills and Competencies

Pragmatists in their basic orientations, the participants assessed their army time in terms of the kind of knowledge provided. Hence, personally useful knowledge gained from the military was discussed with more interest than the impact of the service on civic identity or civic knowledge. In other words, while they afforded little value to the civic knowledge which the army transmitted, they did appreciate the personally relevant knowledge that they had gained. Even though they did not expect the military to have any effect on their personal growth, they were willing to credit it retrospectively with some gains in this realm.

The foremost skill reported was improvement in Hebrew language proficiency. Dimitri provided some insight into this process: "My language ability took a big leap. There were only Israelis there. I could only talk Hebrew, unless I wanted to discuss things with myself. The military gave me a chance to meet Israelis, new people for me whom I really wanted to get to know."

The informants explain their sense of strangeness as stemming from lack of language aptitude, disregarding the existence of intergroup emotional barriers. This is feasible, since they had no aspirations for active social participation, but merely aimed at enhancing their understanding of the new cultural clues from the position of informed bystanders. Katia provided further clarification: "At home I speak Russian, that is home communication. At school, in the military, I spoke Hebrew." The situational use of the two languages sheds light on the divided world of these informants according to audiences and life spheres and could be an asset for globalists. With same-culture peers, they communicated in Russian, even in mixed-culture settings where non-Russian speakers were present. They continued to rely on the normative base of the culture of origin 5 years or more after arriving in the receiving society, even following an intense period of coexistence with local peers in the military.

In addition to increased Hebrew language proficiency, several female participants pointed to an improved sense of self. Irina elaborated:

> I feel I developed in the army. I learnt to be more assertive. I became more independent from my parents. Before, I used to ask my mother when she expected me home. Now I come and go as I please. My father bought me a cell phone so I can call from anywhere. Actually, he bought it for his own peace of mind, not for me.

Gains in self-reliance and self-awareness were also attributed to the service. Dana stated: "I am more secure because of the service, learned about new job opportunities [in civilian life], gained some work experience. I got an idea about things I am good at, something really important I didn't have before." Della said: "Before the army, I thought of myself as unable to communicate. There I discovered I can be open, like to be with people, am accepted by them, even popular. I had lots of doubts and fears. But now I am no longer afraid to try out new things." Some of the female informants emphasized the contribution of these qualities to their present roles as university students. Della explained: "I feel it every day. For example, I have no problem speaking up in class. It doesn't bother me to mispronounce a Hebrew word here and there. I am sure the lecturer gets my point."

On the other hand, those who had been dissatisfied with their army jobs cited no personal gains. Larissa compared her "achievements" with a friend of hers who was not drafted: "In the meantime she earned money. I got nothing, just wasted two years." Vladi tried to present a more balanced picture in spite of his disappointments:

> I had a few nice experiences. Nothing serious. I didn't feel I contributed much, or that I received something meaningful. The service gave me some information on Israel. I learned how to manage the system. The army is a specifically Israeli body and, through it, I found out things about the country and the people. This knowledge helps me sometimes in my everyday life. But nothing really changed in me as a result of the service. I grew older so I am different from what I was three years ago.

His is the only reference to learning at the social systems level though presented as a negative estimate of the reciprocity between himself and the service.

Table 4.1 summarizes the major findings according to the three phases. The columns should be read vertically as each represents specific features characterizing the different time periods.

IN CONCLUSION

Although Israel is among the few immigrant absorbing societies that has mandatory military service, this study found that it did not offer a meaningful context for social integration to the research group. This finding substantiates the conclusions of Azarya and Kimmerling (1983), who contended that while army service helped new immigrants become members of the larger community, it did not facilitate their progression towards the center of society. That study, which was made in the early eighties, based on army released statistics, focused on the attitude of the army towards new immigrant soldiers (without specification of country of origin) as a population with special needs. The present study dealt more with the opposite angle – the subjective perspective of recently released immigrant recruits from a specific cultural background (the FSU), stressing their short- and long-range perceptions of the service.

Analysis of the findings revealed that, while their military service did afford these new immigrants access to Israeli peers, opportunities for friendship and new civic knowledge, the effects of this experience were short-lived, with the exception of the acquisition of personal skills and competencies. Hence, Igor's pre-army expectation that social and cultural integration would take place in the military—an important expectation held by many other immigrant youths from the FSU, quoted at the beginning of this chapter—did not materialize.

The study attempted to consider gender differences in the evaluation of the military service. Indeed, female participants reported experiencing the service more positively. Nonetheless, they too considered the effects of these experiences time-limited in retrospect.

The role of the family, although expected to be restricted (as Igor said, "you can't run home to your parents"), turned out to be prominent. These youth found themselves in the midst of conflicting interests between the army pulling them in and the family refusing to let go. In the final analysis, the prevailing values were found to be those stemming from their culture of origin—promoting separation between public and private and sustaining the belief that the individual is under constant risk of exploitation by officialdom. Many of these views differ vastly from prevailing attitudes in the larger Israeli society, where public-private relations are seen as a continuum (Eisikovits & Karnieli, 1992) and where the

Table 4.1.   Summary of Major Findings by the Three Phases

Before the Draft: *Attitudes to the Service*	*During the Service:* *The Military Experience*	*Aftereffects of* *the Service*
- They saw the civic and the individual as separate in-compatible realms. Considering the army as a public service they perceived it as useless for the individual.	- Several of the male informants' experiences fit the "weathering the storm" and "disappointments" categories according to Lieblich and Perlow's typology.	- Most have not developed a reflective approach about their service.
- Their negative attitudes were reinforced by stories and myths about the Soviet army and its horrors.	- Most female participants can be placed in the positive categories "from fear to mastery" and "hopes fulfilled."	- The tradition of army friendships is a main feature of Israeli society. In contrast, immigrant soldiers severed their military friendships upon the completion of the service.
- A dearth of knowledge about the Israeli army (among parents and recruits) furthered these negative attitudes towards the compulsory service.	- Advancement and change of jobs often only occurred through the intervention and recommendation of their commanders.	- The vast majority of informants seem to support isolationism and differentiation from Israeli civic society, tending to invest little in attempts at acculturation. This lack of effort can be attributed to feelings of alienation and negative predisposition, reinforced by the mixed messages disseminated by the military establishment.
- The army, which was becoming more professional and hence not interested in expanding recruitment, invested little in information dissemination.	- Decreased representation of "integrationist" commanders is bound to result in a cutback in these conscripts' channels for advancement.	
- Interviewees viewed the service as nothing but an obligation (as opposed to veteran Israelis who discuss it in patriotic terms and regard it as an opportunity for recruits' personal development).	- On the overt level, there was no expectation that the army should fulfill individual wishes; as a civic service, it was not expected to be of personal use. Nevertheless, members of both genders appeared to have internalized the orientations of local youths in the military, as a whole, according to satisfaction with their jobs.	- While they afforded little value to the civic knowledge which the army transmitted, they did appreciate the personally relevant knowledge that they had gained, such as improvement in Hebrew language proficiency and gains in self-reliance and self-awareness.

Table continues on next page.

Table 4.1.   Continued

Before the Draft: Attitudes to the Service	During the Service: The Military Experience	Aftereffects of the Service
- Lack of these parents' involvement contrasts with Israeli parents' high involvement and their assistance in their offspring's choice of military jobs.		
- Parents advise conscripts to prefer personal safety and logistic considerations in decisions about army placement, rather than concern for the job itself.		
- No discussions are held about the service at home (compared to ample discussion regarding the army in veteran Israeli homes).		

army has a central position in the population's collective awareness and is widely recognized for its contribution to safeguarding national security.

Most of the informants adopted a minimalist approach towards investment in the service. They concentrated on the formal aspects of the job assigned to them and shut out opportunities for informal social learning that the military offered. Their typical reluctance to be proactive in the service (e.g., not trying to change their jobs if dissatisfied) reinforced their marginality both in the military and in the civil world. They seemed unaware of how this self-seclusion restricted their individual advancement. It should be noted that most participants in this study were young people with high intellectual profiles and considerable chances of career success. Their largely nonreflective view of the service indicates that the army has been a missed opportunity for social integration. But it is also likely to impact on the quality of life of these individuals, who do not recognize the value of social engagement in their new land.

The mismatch between individualistic, passive recruits who are distrustful of bureaucracies and a military in the process of disengaging from its attributed social functions is at the basis of the former's discontent. As long as service in the IDF continues to be compulsory, noninvestment in groups of soldiers with special needs and characteristics is morally indefensible and functionally counterproductive. This research group is part of a sector which constitutes one sixth of the overall population.

Pragmatically, the IDF needs to reconsider its present approach to new immigrants from the FSU, which prepares them solely for the performance of a specific task, leaving them incapable of mobility in the service. The military will not be able to maximize the potential of these draftees unless it better prepares them for the service, providing a broader understanding of the dynamic structure of the military system, with its rules, rights and privileges, and thus helping to dispel their imported stereotypes and overcome their negative attitudes to officialdom. Such an objective requires the establishment of better two-way communication channels with both draftees and their families and a deeper understanding of the immigrants' special problems and hardships. On a wider scale, such investment is likely to positively affect the attitudes of new immigrant soldiers. Continued nonaction only serves to justify ongoing resistance to the civic apparatus which, in turn, reinforces isolationist tendencies.

Having considered how the military can improve its functioning vis-à-vis immigrant recruits, let us now turn to insights gained concerning the likelihood of these youths' becoming successful globalists. On the basis of this study it is mixed. The strong parental influence yields sturdy ethnocultural roots which enhance potential for mobility and global participation. Nonetheless, a question arises as to their amenability to change due to these intense intergenerational ties, that is, their impact on creativity and capacity for cross-cultural collaboration. No querying of beliefs and customs formed in and brought along from the country of origin was noted. One of the outcomes is constant analysis of the new system according to parameters developed in the old one which inevitably leads to inappropriate conclusions and, often, to self-defeating actions. A conspicuous example is the sharp distinction between public and private, shown to have barred them from taking personal advantage of the informal sources of learning and support the service had to offer. On the other hand, ethnic versus territorial attachment is a promobility trait, as is their natural skill to operate on situationally-based identities.

NOTES

1. Currently, 3 years for young men and 20 months for young women.
2. Exemptions are granted to various groups: young women on grounds of the family of origin's traditional life style or an early marriage; orthodox young men studying in religious institutions of higher learning and certain categories of new immigrants. See Cohen (1994, pp. 237–254).
3. The interviews were performed by a research team which, in addition to myself, as principal investigator, comprised eight female graduate students trained in qualitative research methods. Six of them had served in the army, two as officers. The students, Y. Assoulin, N. Ben-Rachamim, Y.

Chen, L. Erez, Z. Goldstein, O. Gur-Arieh, Y. Hadar, and E. Shai, participated in my research seminar: "Education in a Multicultural Society." Their contribution to data collection is acknowledged. As in the study reported upon in chapter three, I am solely responsible for data analysis and write-up.

4.   As noted earlier, there are grounds on which females can be released, but the informants ignore many of the service conditions.

5.   Israeli males perform army reserve duty up to 30 days per year, usually until the age of 30.

6.   For a comparison see Segal and Kestenbaum (2002, pp. 441–458),

PART II

(DO) WE LISTEN

CHAPTER 5

"THEY DO EXCEL, THE TROUBLE IS THEY COME IN AS RUSSIANS AND LEAVE AS RUSSIANS FOUR YEARS LATER"

Teaching High-Achieving Transnationalists

There is general agreement that cultural diversity has become a global challenge to public education. In the United States minority students are estimated to constitute one-third of the public school population (Banks, 2001). In Europe the dilemmas concerning the best way to handle the high percentage of children of immigrants in formal educational settings has been the top issue on the recent educational research agenda of the Council of Europe (Eldering & Kloprogge, 1989; Figueroa, 1995). This is equally true in Australia where in addition to indigenous aborigines, making up more than 1% of the total population, about 25% of inhabitants was born overseas (Allan & Hill, 1995).

The magnitude of the challenge not withstanding, systematic training of teachers in multicultural education is in short supply (Banks, 2001;

Immigrant Youth Who Excel: Globalization's Uncelebrated Heroes, pp. 97–116
Copyright © 2008 by Information Age Publishing
All rights of reproduction in any form reserved.

Frankrijker, 1997; Shamai & Paul-Binyamin, 2004; Tatar & Horenczyk, 2003). Hence, working with culturally diverse student populations is often considered an added burden to the teacher's already heavy workload, indeed a stressor, referred to at times as a source of teacher burnout (Macdonald, 1999; Tatar & Horenczyk, 2003). The underlying assumption of this line of thinking is that culturally diverse students are disadvantaged because of their ethno-cultural background, which is at the root of their lower academic achievement (Gibson, 1988; Kibria, 2003; Portes & Rumbaut, 2001; Waldinger & Feliciano, 2004). In addition, teachers are generally seen as lacking the skill and specific knowledge necessary to successfully handle multicultural classes (Shamai & Paul-Binyamin, 2004; Taylor & Sobel, 2001; Zhou, 2003). If they do receive any training it usually concentrates on ways to handle the lower tiers, for example, culturally diverse students who face difficulties crossing the barriers presented by the school due to lack of effective dialogue between their home cultures and that of the school.

The picture that emerges from the present study, based on semistructured interviews with 40 Israeli high-school teachers working with culturally heterogeneous student populations is more positive. Although studies documenting high achieving culturally diverse student groups abound (Rumbaut & Portes, 2001; Xie & Goyette, 2004; Zhou & Xiong, 2005), little attention has been paid to teacher attitudes toward such students and treatment of them. This study focuses on the experience of Israeli teachers who tell the story of a decade and a half of educational work with highly motivated, academically successful immigrant students from the Former Soviet Union (FSU).

In their research on diversity-related teacher burnout Tatar and Horenczyk (2003) conducted a quantitative investigation of 280 primary and secondary school Israeli teachers who worked with a similar student population. But there are two major differences between their study and the present one, aside from the methodological one. First, Tatar and Horenczyk do not distinguish teacher responses according to their subject matter area (humanities vs. mathematics/science), whereas the present study assumed that teacher experiences are intensely affected by their subject matter area. Second, Tatar and Horenczyk assume the "difficulty of the clients" and assess Russian students by "misbehavior" categories gleaned from the literature (Borg, Riding, & Falzon, 1991; Burke & Greenglass, 1993; Byrne, 1994; McCormick, 1997). In their words, "students' misbehavior is one of the major causes of stress, as reported by teachers. It includes students' noisy behavior, impoliteness, poor attitudes towards school work, discipline problems, lack of motivation, apathy and low achievements" (Tatar & Horenczyk, 2003, p. 398). None of these misbehavior descriptors apply to the student population of the present study.

Participating teachers did not consider these youngsters to be "difficult clients," indeed the majority regarded teaching them to be a prize.

THE STUDY

The research focused on 40 female teachers[1] in public high schools in the Northern City metropolitan area,[2] working with 16–18-year-old students in culturally heterogeneous classrooms with 20% Russian immigrant students (*Ris*). Participants were selected through "snowball sampling" (Dane, 1990). The research group consisted of four equal subgroups established by subject matter (humanities versus mathematics/sciences)[3] and seniority (up to 7 years in the profession vs. more than 7 years).

In the first stage of the research, open-ended pilot interviews were conducted with four additional teachers who served as key informants for the four subgroups. From the analysis of these interviews four central themes emerged: experience versus expectations; dealing with *Ris* academically; dealing with *Ris* socially; and reflections on the job of teaching *Ris*. These were the broad topics addressed in the semistructured interviews that followed.[4] All interviews were content-analyzed using cultural domain analysis. A cultural domain is a category of cultural meaning (See Borgatti, 1993; Dressler, Borges, Balieiro, & dos Santos, 2005; Spradley, 1979 for a broader treatment of the topic). The teachers agreed to participate in the study in the hope that the interviews would provide an opportunity to think through some unresolved issues in their day-to-day work with the students.

EXPERIENCE VERSUS EXPECTATIONS

Expectations about the immigrant students stemmed from stereotypes and were divided into concerns about behavior and subject matter or content know-how. When asked to reconstruct her feelings about the first time she noticed Russian names on the list of her students, Dina, a veteran teacher of literature said: "I was afraid of physical fights between them and the other students. They had a very negative image." The source of Dina's fear is not clear, other than cumulative teacher experience with various groups of immigrant students who were supposed to exhibit problems of conduct because of communication difficulties and cultural disorientation. In reality Dina's *Ris* turned out to be anything but rowdy: "I got to know them and realized they were cooperative right from the beginning." The juxtaposition between her two statements came to highlights the dichotomy between negative expectations and positive experience.

Some veteran teachers of humanities (*vth*), like Dina, emphasized student originated difficulties as expected sources of problems, others expressed doubts about their own ability to cope with them. Simona explained:

> Maybe I won't get through to them. Maybe there will be obstacles I won't manage to overcome, personal ones. That's the real worry I had. In spite of the fact that I have a way with students I was uncertain that it would work with them.

If *vth*-s were concerned with general behavior problems despite their years of experience, junior teachers of humanities (*jth*) were even more worried. The latter, however, expected difficulties related to subject matter in the immediate area of instructional work. Malka, a junior teacher of literature noted: "My concerns were about the students' mastery of Hebrew. How will I teach grammar to youngsters who don't know the language?" But *vth*-s and *jth*-s alike were reassured as both types of negative expectations turned out to be ungrounded.

The expectations of humanities and mathematics teachers proceeded in opposite directions. Whereas humanities teachers started with fears and negative expectations and became favorably surprised by their face-to-face encounters with the immigrant students, mathematics teachers started with positive stereotypes and ended up being disappointed. Aviva, a veteran teacher of mathematics (*vtm*) said: "The myth is that they are good mathematicians. When I meet one who is not I ask what went wrong?" Pnina, also a *vtm*, put it bluntly:

> Because of the exceptional reputation Russians have in mathematics I said to myself well, I am lucky. I saw three Russian names on my register and I was convinced I will get three outstanding students. I thought we were headed toward glorious days in mathematics education. But actually no more than 10–15% were top students; quite similar to the proportion among our regular students; it's not a flood of geniuses.

Neither veteran nor junior mathematics teachers (*jtm*) expected behavioral problems. "Mathematicians are disciplined people," remarked Einath, a *jtm*. But the two groups differed considerably in their attitudes towards these students.

DEALING WITH *RIS* ACADEMICALLY

The overall attitude of the *vth*-s was enthusiastic. Impressed with their students' study skills, the teachers were more excited to work with these students than were the other three groups. According to Jaffa, a literature teacher: "One can tell them by their calligraphy. Also their sentence structure is distinctive. They are visibly translating from another language, but their writing is more mature." Ilana, a Hebrew language teacher, said: "When I take a Russian student's paper in my hand I know ahead of time it will be good. No hallow effect. You know, language like math is a precise field. Answers are either right or wrong." Teachers were impressed by the students' serious attitude toward school and studying, by their interest in literature, and by their ability to "read the [Russian] classics in the original language," as Ruchama, a veteran teacher of literature put it. These teachers made every effort to help the students with their language difficulties. Ruchama continued:

> These kids are hungry for help. Their motivation is higher than what we are used to. I am willing to come and work extra hours with them. If a teacher is looking for pleasure in her job—it is with them. They corrected my pronunciation of Russian names when I taught stories by Chekhov. They even drew my attention to short stories by him I was not aware of, and believe me I know this stuff inside out.

The *vth-s* were the only group that conceded to have made changes in their teaching style as a result of this intercultural encounter. These senior teachers had the self-confidence to admit the need for a change and perceived it as an indication of personal development. Several acknowledged preparing for classes more thoroughly owing to the intelligent questions these students asked. This is a surprising finding because the logic of the situation is not conducive to this teacher perception. In a language-dependent subject, such as literature, immigrant students are not expected to boost the learning process. This perception illustrates that teacher openness is required to recognize the inherent resources dwelling in cultural diversity.

Although *jth*-s also expressed a positive disposition for working with *Ris*, most of them confessed not to have thought about the issue before the interview; a surprising finding in view of the increased emphasis on pluralism in the public discourse. Nevertheless, this emphasis did not translate into systematic multicultural training in teacher education (Yogev, 1996; Shamai & Paul-Benjamin, 2004). Indeed, several participants complained about a lack of preparation in preservice and in-service teacher training forums. Furthermore, they pointed out the absence of organizational arrangements in the schools to face these problems.

Consequently, the interviews with the *jth*-s were characterized by ideological confusion. Informants often voiced pluralistic claims and illustrated them with mismatched homogenized practices. For example, Ilana said: "I respect them the way they are, and relate to them according to their seriousness, specific needs, and ambitions. In other words, I try to treat all my students fairly and equally."

By contrast, the *vth*-s were trained under the assimilationist ideology of nation building prevalent in the Israeli educational system in the first two decades of independent statehood (Eisikovits, 1997). They continued to practice along these same lines, with a professional self-perception of cultural transmitters (see chapter 6 for a discussion of this topic). Shoshana, for instance, interpreted attending to culturally based needs in the following way:

> I feel the same responsibility for the success of all my students. You (the interviewer) are asking me particularly about my behavior according to the students' origin. But I don't differentiate them by this criterion. I have no preference for Russian or local Israeli students.

Unlike the *vth*-s who had a clear ideology (culturally sensitive or not), a wealth of personal experience, and self-confidence to rely upon, the *jth*-s felt the magnitude of the challenge. But because they did not problematize working with the *Ris*, the challenge never came to be defined as a burden. In their view, the great majority of *Ris* were academically successful and nonproblematic from the point of view of behavior. In the absence of specific professional tools to deal with the *Ris*, ignoring differences between immigrant and local students was the junior teachers' best option. Their lack of reflectiveness regarding the treatment of the *Ris* can be considered a defense mechanism.

Seniority did not produce qualitative distinctions between the two groups of humanities teachers on this issue. Thus, rather than recognizing culture-based differential needs, both groups proceeded to redefine situations and sources of problems by various tactics of difference minimization to make similarities with the general student body more prominent and defensible. This enabled them to apply uniform approaches to all their students, immigrant and local alike. The veterans employed a mixture of assimilationist ideology and egalitarian professional ethics to underpin their homogenizing practices, whereas the juniors' "egalitarianism" stemmed from considerations of convenience. They felt less personally responsible for the welfare of the *Ris*, considering it to be the exclusive duty of specific role incumbents, such as homeroom teachers or student counselors. On the whole, they were more narrowly role oriented, and their perception of these students was limited to classroom interaction. In contrast, the *vth*-s were willing to go much farther. Liat clarified: "I see them as people with life stories, not just as students in my class." Despite these differences both groups considered it a professional challenge to work with such serious students.

Whereas humanities teachers ignored the need for culturally based differential treatment of their students owing to social or professional ideologies or to simple pragmatism, mathematics teachers found the rationale for their "egalitarianism" in the subject matter itself. "Mathematics is a universal language in which local terms in Hebrew or Russian play a minor role," Hava observed.

The *vtm*-s tended to adopt a microlevel technical approach to immigrant students' needs. They categorized them by the mathematics track to which they were assigned and looked upon them through the administrative steps that their tracking required. Shlomit indicated: "Only a small fraction of immigrant students made it to the five-credit track. I was not aware of their immigrant status because they did not need any special allowances." Miriam pointed out: "I don't pay attention to students' names." This was provided as proof of her nonbiased attitude toward students. Some teachers in this group conceptualized work with *Ris* in the context of a large variety of special needs students—yet another form of homogenization. In this case "special needs" may have meant the need for a few more words of explanation. Using an organizational *we* rather than a personal *I* was common among these teachers. Michal, for example, said: "We are told about students with special needs by the counselor," meaning that it is not the responsibility of subject matter teachers, and certainly not that of any individual *vtm*. Considerable emphasis was placed in the interviews on clarifying the routine school treatment of these students. Nechama described: "We send them to an *Ulpan* first. Only then do they join our regular classes, so they can follow our explanations. We try to have a math teacher in charge of the *Ulpan* class." The last statement came to stress the importance of the subject matter. In other words, no time should be wasted if one wishes to succeed in mathematics.

The *vtm*-s were less excited about these students than were the *vth*-s, and tended not to recognize their excellence as being group specific. It seems that such recognition would have threatened their professional prestige, that is, it would have underscored their responsibility for the relatively lower level of the local students. Thus, they emphatically pointed out that the Russian students' excellence was myth rather than reality, and that the percentage of outstanding individuals among them is comparable to that among Israeli students. This is an unexpected finding. One would expect these senior teachers to be inclined to foster their talented immigrant students, but the perceived threat to professional status outweighed the commitment to the pursuit of excellence.

The attitude among the *jtms* was different. Members of this group were willing to acknowledge these students' imported skills (Pearson, 1990) and distinguished performance, and were prepared to invest time and energy in their advancement. As Yonit put it: "I am a new teacher and I want to succeed in my job. It's clear to me that their success is my success. I'll do anything to maximize their potential." Having less accrued reputation and therefore less to protect, they considered themselves staunch promoters of the universal mathematical genius as personified by the *Ris*.

DEALING WITH *RIS* SOCIALLY

Discipline

Although the teachers' general claim was that the *Ris* did not present disciplinary concerns, closer scrutiny revealed behavioral aberrations that the teachers construed as cultural misunderstandings fueled by liminality. As a result, respondents related to them as temporary manifestations and tried to explain them away. Daniela, a *vth*, told the following story:

> I had a case of a boy in my class [where she served as homeroom teacher] who approached the computer right in front of the teacher, disconnected it, cut off the plug, and put it in his pocket. To the teacher's amazement he responded dryly: "I need one of these at home." The teacher asked him if he would have proceeded this way in Russia, as well. His answer was: "No, in Russia I wouldn't have done it but here everyone does whatever he pleases." Astonishing! A clear case of misreading the rules of the game. He was not trying to steal. He did what he did openly, no attempt to hide his act. He did not think anything was wrong. To the question how he thought the computer would work, he answered: "The technician will fix it. I saw he has a lot of plugs in his lab." This was an extreme example but they often mistake the free spirit in our schools for anarchy. I guess they are also testing our limits.

Gabriela pointed out additional visible expressions of such misreadings, this time in the girls' conduct:

> Girls also reacted bizarrely, wearing exaggerated makeup and hair color to school. It's easily available so at the beginning they would overdo it. They looked cheap and out of place, were simply dazzled by this abundance. Their slogan was: "In Russia I wouldn't have appeared like this but here it's a free country." I tried to explain that in our lexicon this is vulgar behavior, not a manifestation of freedom, and that it shows them in a very bad light.

But the counterbalancing statement was soon to follow as Gabriela went on:

> Yet these girls are so polite. When I ask one or the other to meet me during the break for a one-on-one, the question usually is: "Who's going to call you from the teachers lounge?" They can't imagine going in there. They have respect for teachers and wouldn't ask for personal assistance with any problem outside the classroom unless I offered it myself.

An additional balancing example brought up by Carmela, a *jtm*, paid tribute to the fact that "they won't ever try to negotiate, as local students often do, over the date of an exam."

Another attempt to rationalize nonnormative behavior, also culturally induced, emphasized their initial socialization to a different teacher-student relationship in their country of origin. In view of this experience they were believed to misinterpret the open style of Israeli teachers. Adi explained: "Their behavior has to do with a lack of ability to get along with teachers who are not authoritative. Their type of teacher is distant and autocratic. That causes a lot of friction." Absenteeism was also ascribed a social explanation. "A serious problem among *Ris*, much worse than among *Sabras*, is absenteeism. Many of them work to avoid having to ask their parents for allowances," Yifat said. Most often parents are unaware of this phenomenon and the teachers refrain from bringing it to their attention for two reasons: they believe that these young people are mature enough to talk it over with them; and they fear the parents' harsh reactions. Ora elucidated:

> I talk to the students themselves. They respond when they realize that the teachers care about them personally. I turn to the parents as a last resort. There were cases of violence. Parents think their kids went to school and are furious to find out they were not there.

These cultural accounts were supplied by the *vth-s*, who seemed most interested in their students' welfare. Not surprisingly the majority of homeroom teachers belonged to this group. Assimilationist Ravit, an outspoken teacher of literature, provided the following insight: "I see how they struggle, how difficult it is for them to cope. When a Russian kid violates some rule it makes me feel pleased inside. I take it as a sign of adjustment." Junior teachers tried to steer clear of such responsibility for reasons described earlier.

Regardless of seniority, teachers of mathematics met *Ris* in small homogeneous groups because mathematics teaching is tracked. Due to this instructional format, they were less exposed to behavioral problems.

"No trouble with conduct. In these advanced tracks they are too busy catching up with the material," Sara remarked.

In general, the topic of discipline was summed up in highly favorable terms. Teachers perceived them as reverent of school standards and regulations and reciprocated with respect toward the students. An overall sense of mutuality permeated these relationships.

Separatism

One concern that teachers of all levels of seniority and disciplinary background voiced was the separatism of *Ris*. Miri, a *vth*, complained: "They were a separate group 15 years ago and they still are today." Tamar, a *jth*, put it more dramatically: "They come in as Russians and they leave as Russians four years later. They are invisible. Last year nobody wrote about any of them in the anniversary book. They would not even have their pictures taken." Their interactions with their peer group in the host society and their effect on the school culture were on the whole, negligible. Sivan, a *jth*, said:

> They stick to their own ways, speak Russian, and don't interact with the outside world. At most, they exchange a notebook with an Israeli student, a few casual words. They are busy erecting walls around themselves. No curiosity. As if they were not living here. The local kids get tired, give up.

The *vth*-s who invested in them beyond the call of duty showed a negative emotional reaction to this separatist attitude. Some took it personally and viewed it as their failure to reach out to them. Varda explained:

> I know how hard it must be to arrive in a new country. If I had to do it I'd be terrified. This is why I wanted to cushion their entry. I invited them to my house for cookies and hot chocolate and went on home visits, but couldn't hit it off with them. They wouldn't open up to me.

Others brought up personal experiences from their own adolescence as new immigrants. Dvora shared: "I told them that I also came as a new immigrant at their age and how I suffered from loneliness, how I wanted to be included. I tried to explain that it's a two way street, but didn't see any initiative on their part."

Whereas on the issue of discipline interviewees reported a reciprocal harmonious relationship, isolationism elicited discordant reactions from members of the same group because of the perceived imbalance between their input and the students' response. For example, students declined to participate in extracurricular activities such as school trips or parties despite the homeroom teachers' efforts to persuade school administration to exempt them from incurred expenses. Nevertheless, the *vth*-s provided culturally based excuses for them in these matters, as well. Dina indicated: "They are not used to these things. There were no school organized trips or parties in Russia. For these youngsters school and fun don't go together. As for community volunteering, that brings up really bad memories." Teachers found another clue for this separatist tendency in the parents' emphasis on the academic aspect of schooling: "Who could blame them?! That is only natural when people distrust the system and fear Soviet brain washing of their children," Simona noted.

Teacher attitudes toward culturally diverse students is generally described as lacking the necessary cultural sensitivity to maximize the students' potential. This is often considered to be the root cause of these students' lower academic achievement (Perlman & Waldinger, 1997; Portes & Rumbaut, 2001; Zhou, 1997). In this case, contrary to the literature cited above, the immigrant students exhibit high academic achievements and possess study skills that have earned them their teachers' admiration. But the assimilationist teachers, mostly *vth-s*, were at a loss trying to account for their students' seclusionist behavior. Israeli teachers' experience with culturally diverse students relies mainly on groups of low achievers, such as the children of the immigration waves from African and Asian countries during the 1950s or from Ethiopia during the 1980s (Eisikovits, 1997). They have no working models for handling culturally diverse students in such high proportions who are successful academically despite their resistance to assimilate into the receiving society.

All attempts at intercultural approximation initiated by the teachers were personal, for lack of professional training. As a result, the reaction to failure was also personal, expressed in emotional terms of anger or hurt. In Yaffa's words:

> We try to respect their traditions. One of the teachers told me that she planned an exam for the first of January. Two Russian immigrant girls came up to her complaining they had a problem because they celebrate the New Year [which in Israel is not an official holiday] and can't attend. They were serious and committed students so the teacher postponed the exam.

Yet, the teachers' expectations of mutuality were not met. Yaffa continued: "On Memorial Day they took the day off as if the ceremony did not concern them. This made me real angry."

The orientation of the *jth*-s was guided by organizational rumors. Hearsay about the frustrations of the *vth*-s reinforced their noninvolvement. At the same time, there were those who saw in the students' separatism a means of reciprocal help. Mathematics teachers, mostly the junior ones, held this view. Adina observed: "At times they cause some disturbance because they chat among themselves. Mostly it is because they try to clear language problems, explain things to each other."

The emotional state of the *vth*-s, as described above, turned out to be a temporary stage, to be transcended and replaced by the realization that separatism was a survival mechanism for these youngsters. They realized that *Ris* had unique and specific problems that could not be discussed outside the group of same-culture peers. Eventually, the teachers perceived the students' separatism as being thrust upon them by their existential predicament rather than chosen as a willful act. This perception paved the way for the assimilationist teachers to assume the role of saviors. Ravit explained: "I feel it's a challenge, a mission for each of us to do our share and more than that. The parents are busy with subsistence, and the kids have no one to turn to. I want to open doors for them, see to it that they have a brighter future." Their attitude, still emotional, transformed into one of identification with the students' hardships. Meital expressed it in compelling terms: "of course there is a change in my attitude to *Ris* since I have been working with them. It's not an abstract issue for me. It's not something you see on TV or read about in the paper. It became personal. It has a face."

According to these teachers, Russian students were socialized to keep family issues private and set up clear boundaries between home and school. "Teachers were seen as part of the system. Therefore one was not expected to share personal matters with them," Miri noted. *Ris* are believed to have brought along this principle and applied it to teachers in the receiving society. She added: "We learn about serious problems, such as parents' illness, hospitalization, and other sorts of trouble much later and always from a secondary source." Economic hardships were also not discussed, as Ruchama pointed out:

> They have lots of family problems, economic problems, single parent families, kids who come with their grandparents. Can you imagine a teenager immigrating without parents? Parents divorce, remarry. These are strong kids with lots of will power.

Teachers learned to value the sense of self-reliance of *Ris* and their personal pride, and were encouraged by the fact that students gradually responded to their unrelenting concern. Simona said: "I stay in class during breaks; ask about their outside activities; try to get to know them. Slowly they begin to trust me. It takes time and patience. This type of care from teachers is unfamiliar in these circles." Although the *vth*-s recognized that Russian students had a different mindset than their Israeli peers, it became clear that the assimilationist saviors knew no other way of approaching them.

REFLECTIONS ON THE JOB OF TEACHING *RIS*

Teacher dispositions toward their work with *Ris* ranged from no reflection before the interview (*jth*-s), through a minimalistic technical approach (*vtm*-s) and task-oriented flexibility (*jtm*-s), to deep commitment (*vth*-s). Perceptions of the need for change in teaching styles as a result of work experience with these high achievers varied accordingly. The *vtm*-s were of the opinion that the minor assistance with language difficulties that immigrant students required presupposed no instructional adaptation on their part. The *jtm*-s, though flexible, were nonspecific. Their orientation could be termed open-ended and eclectic. Einat conceded: "I would be willing to try practically any method with them. They are talented and worth the trouble." The *jth*-s' position, if one could so designate an admittedly nonreflective stance, was best summed up by Malka: "They are good students, so why should I change anything in my way of teaching?" According to this approach, only underachievement due to cultural diversity warrants teacher adaptation. Mentoring of excellence among culturally diverse students was not perceived to necessitate instructional adjustments by these teachers. As noted, only members of the *vth* group admitted having made such a change and spoke enthusiastically about the effect of this intercultural encounter on their personal and professional experience. Simona related: "They read, although in Russian, are interested. I use simple language because of them, but the ideas are more complex. All in all, I feel I became a better teacher because of the stimulation they provide."

Teachers underlined the importance of personal experience as a source of knowledge in the absence of systematic training in multicultural education. In his discussion of the importance of craft for the professional development of teachers, Shimahara (1998, p. 451) calls attention to the centrality of "perpetuating occupational practices from the past" to salvage this "accumulated wisdom." He maintains that "craft knowledge is embedded in teachers' lives and teachers promote professional development through in-service education that creates and reproduces the culture of teaching by sharing ideas, skills, beliefs and practical innovations" (p. 459). But despite the experience of 15 years of work with *Ris*, participants, particularly the *vth*-s, did not feel in possession of such wisdom. The reason is that they deemed themselves unsuccessful in their social mission, that is, the assimilation of *Ris*, which to them seemed more vital than furthering the students' academic achievements.

Table 5.1 provides a summary of both general and group-dependent positions on the central topics discussed.

CONCLUDING COMMENTS

Table 5.1 graphically illustrates the kaleidoscopic picture of teacher perceptions of their work with this academically successful group of culturally diverse students, broken down by seniority and subject matter. Although I chose teachers with strong and clear voices as spokespersons for the various groups, in fact, I found surprisingly low within-group variation, which corroborates the high impact of these categories on teachers' opinion formation.

Despite the shared recognition for the virtues of *Ris*, expressed by participants of each group in their own fashion, and despite reports of favorable experiences in working with them, little effective communication was observed between teachers and students. Since the deepest chasm was apparent in the relationship with the *vth-s*, I chose to focus on the dynamics between this committed group of teachers and the *Ris* in my concluding remarks. These ties were characterized by mutual misunderstanding of the other side's role and expectations. No possibility for genuine dialogue was structurally feasible because each party ignored the other's ground rules and acted in direct opposition to them. The miscommunication sprang from the fundamental clash between the students' transnationalist tendencies (Glick-Schiller, Basch, & Blanc-Szanton, 1995; Lewellen, 2002; Vertovec, 2001) and the *vth-s*' nation building orientation. Transnationalist Russian immigrants tend to regard the heritage of their country of origin as their cultural epicenter. In a survey of 800 Russian Israelis Remennick (2002) shows that the culturally retentive inclination holds true for the younger generation as well. She claims that:

> Young people who immigrated at high school age and above are almost as determined to remain "Russians" as are their parents. Although they master Hebrew rather quickly and generally do well in school and in college, their informal social networks remain mainly co-ethnic. (p. 525)

Exponents of the nation-building trend of thought, the *vth-s* could not fathom the mechanism of academic success despite social separatism. It contradicted their ingrained belief that high scholastic achievement of culturally diverse students was contingent upon assimilation into the receiving society's cultural mainstream and acceptance by the host culture peer group. In other words, the teachers were stumped by the coexistence of excellence with cultural isolationism. In their experience, cultural

Table 5.1. Teachers' Positions According to Seniority and Subject Matter Grouping

Theme	General	Veteran Teachers of Humanities	Junior Teachers of Humanities	Veteran Teachers of Mathematics	Junior Teachers of Mathematics
Expectations vs. experience		- Were concerned about generalized behavioral problems - Favorably surprising—as negative expectations turned out to be ungrounded	- Feared difficulties related to subject matter instruction - Favorably surprising—as both types of expectations turned out to be ungrounded	- High—based on positive stereotypes regarding Russian students' mathematical skills - Disappointing—as found *Ris* were not more talented than local students	- Favorable—as recognized *Ris*' talents
Dealing with *Ris* academically	- Redefined sources of *Ris*' difficulties through various tactics of difference minimization to warrant uniform approach to the entire student body	- Enthusiastic about *Ris*' academic skills, motivation and serious attitude to studying - Clear-cut assimilationist ideology translated into fitting egalitarian practice - Based on ideological grounds	- Positive disposition to work with *Ris*, though confessed not to have had a defined stance on the issue - Ideological confusion in treatment of *Ris*: pluralistic stance accompanied by unmatching homogenized practice - Based on pragmatic grounds	- Minimized their excellence as group specific due to risk to own professional prestige - Based on the universalist nature of the subject matter	- Were ready to invest in their promotion as it coincided with own professional goals

Table continues on next page.

Table 5.1. Continued

Theme	General	Veteran Teachers of Humanities	Junior Teachers of Humanities	Veteran Teachers of Mathematics	Junior Teachers of Mathematics
Dealing with Ris socially Discipline	- Regarded behavioral problems as temporary, attributing them to cultural misunderstandings - Perceived Ris as reverent of school regulations, hence returned them respect	- Served as homeroom teachers and took a broad interest in their welfare	- Expressed limited, strictly classroom level interest in Ris		- Met Ris in small groups since math teaching is tracked, therefore were less exposed to behavioral problems
Separation	- Viewed it as the most problematic feature of work with Ris	- At stage one—negative emotional reaction; interpreted it as own failure to reach out to Ris - At stage two—realized it was due to their existential predicament - At stage three—identified with Ris' hardships, as a result turned into "assimilationist saviors"	- Minimally involved in dealing with Ris' social issues	- No opinion on the subject	- Disregarding the social aspect, related to it as an enhancer of reciprocal help in the subject matter among same culture peers

	Deep commitment	No reflection prior to interview	Minimalist technical approach	Flexible task orientation
Reflections on the job of teaching *Ris* Disposition toward work with *Ris*				
Need for change in teaching method to adapt to needs of immigrant students	- Admitted such change due to this intercultural encounter; spoke zealously about its effect on their professional development	- High achievement among culturally diverse students does not warrant teacher adaptation	- No need for change in teaching style due to the minimal assistance these students required	- Eclectic orientation—ready to try out various methods to help *Ris*, considered them worth the effort
- For lack of systematic multicultural training relied on personal experience as main source of knowledge				

diversity necessarily led to underachievement. Hence, these teachers were unequipped to satisfy the needs of the *Ris*.

Although the essence of transnationalism is not discussed theoretically, it is amply experienced in countless realms of Israeli civic life. Unfamiliar with this concept, the general public interprets its manifestations as a threat to national unity because of the large size of the Russian immigrant population (Remennick, 2002). The educational system turns a blind eye to it, as demonstrated by the inaction that extends from the policymaking level down to that of teachers' day-to-day realities. The absence of guidelines for coping with this new type of cultural diversity is yet another sign of the complete bafflement of the educational establishment with this phenomenon. As a result participants in this study were stuck at the stage of diagnosing their students' seclusionism, with no plan for moving outside their own assimilationsist routine. The less emotionally involved *jth*-s noted various symptoms of cultural superiority underlying the separatist conduct of the *Ris*. Lilit noted: "Sometimes I feel they treat us like natives." But for the *vth*-s such an insight would have undermined their tenacious adhesion to their position of assimilationist saviors. Analysis of the interviews indicates that a decade and a half of work experience with these students produced no change in teachers' comprehension of the issue.

Teacher attitudes and educational approaches towards high achieving immigrant students have not been studied. No research has been conducted on the analysis of such attitudes and approaches based on subject matter area and years of experience. Therefore it is my suggestion that the critical reader relate heuristically to the experience of the four teacher categories portrayed in this study and learn about the various problem solving methods, omissions, instances of cultural communication and miscommunication that characterized their modus operandi. Reflecting upon analogous situations that might occur in one's own educational context and practice, in light of these experiences, could be rewarding. Nothing is more economical and less threatening than self-edification through contemplation of others' deeds and misdeeds. A few illustrative questions arising from this material follow:

- Is there room for adaptations in teaching styles to cater to the needs of high achieving immigrant students; if so, how should they be implemented?
- Do tactics of disregarding the specific interests of such students— due to possible lack of sufficient preparation in multicultural education—constitute pitfalls that might occur in one's own practice; if so, how could one minimize them?

- Under what circumstances would teachers incline to ignore differences between immigrant and local students?
- Whom does fake homogenization of the student body serve and whom does it harm; in what ways?
- What role does the teacher's professional status play in the decision to recognize the academic excellence of his/her immigrant students and promote it?
- Attempts to find cultural explanations for behavioral problems among such students—do they necessarily serve the latter's needs; under what conditions would they be likely to achieve that end?
- How do various teachers construct their particular interpretations of a certain behavioral pattern manifested by their high achieving immigrant students?
- What part do ideologies that teachers live by play in their dealings with their high achieving immigrant students?
- How can teachers' personal experiences be utilized to enhance intercultural communication with such students?

The potential for multidirectional enrichment that this type of intercultural encounter can yield, illustrated partially in this in-depth study, remains to be more fully explored. As globalization expends, with multitudes of international experts, high-tech specialists, academics, and others on the move, culturally and ethnically retentive transnationalist students, like the *Ris* portrayed in this study, will become an increasingly conspicuous presence in schools of the future the world over. Educators will be confronted with this new form of cultural diversity and should learn to discern the unique characteristics of these students to bring out their assets. Fruitful collaboration between local students and talented young immigrants present myriad opportunities for mutual enhancement which educators should foster. Multicultural teacher trainers should pay attention to this phenomenon and address it systematically, in both preservice and in-service contexts. In lack of such concerted efforts, schools, as we know them, will become irrelevant in preparing the young for global participation.

NOTES

1.   Teaching is a female dominated profession. About 75% of the teachers in Israel are women (Addi-Raccah, 2005).
2.   The Northern City metropolitan area houses one of the largest concentrations of immigrants from the FSU, who constitute 30–40% of the

population in certain neighborhoods. The large wave of migration from this part of the world during the 1990s brought in approximately one million people, a number which makes up one-fifth of the state's Jewish population. One million Arabs, belonging to various religious denominations, account for the rest of the country's seven million citizens.

3.   In the two mathematics/science subgroups the great majority of participants were teachers of mathematics. Therefore I refer to them as such from here on.

4.   The contribution of the following graduate students who assisted me with data collection is acknowledged: H. Avni, L. Ben-Shlomo, H. Fisher, A. Manzur, S. Nissim, D. Ohana, M. Rosales, T. Shaul, and L. Shavit.

CHAPTER 6

"THE QUESTION IS WHERE TO PLACE THE *ULPAN* CLASS"

Diverging Approaches to the Education of Immigrants

International migration is a common feature of modern global life, nevertheless, attitudes of host countries to immigrants vary from tolerance to enthusiastic support or even active solicitation depending on underlying rationales. Though an issue in its own right, the educational treatment of immigrant children is influenced by these considerations. Granted that schools carry out social mandates, clashes between educational goals, which are by definition long range, and short-range economic interests that promote immigration, still occur. Thus, schools become battlefields in wars they have not started.

In spite of being a topic of high interest to host societies, a survey of the literature reveals that in many countries the bulk of writing consists of statements of national educational goals spelled out in terms of policy or curriculum guidelines (Crul, 2007; McAndrew, 2007). Less attention has been devoted to the task of deciphering educational systems level processes related to migration. In other words, how actual schools deal with immigrant students as part of their everyday routine. This is what I

Immigrant Youth Who Excel: Globalization's Uncelebrated Heroes, pp. 117–135

undertake in this chapter; that is, present an ethnographic account of five such settings—two elementary and three high schools—in the northern part of Israel known to be working intensively with new immigrant students (NIS). Through the perspectives of various role incumbents, the study explores and compares the effectiveness of their approaches to handling NIS. It is my belief that such a contextualized analysis permits a broad appraisal of goals and means and that these inductively derived models of educational practice provide operational translations of professed ideologies.[1]

Israel is at the positive end of the spectrum of known attitudes toward immigrants. The Zionist emphasis on nation building through the "ingathering of exiles" codified in the "law of return," the first constitutional law of the State of Israel, shows the value placed on immigration. Its educational dimension is an intrinsic interest in immigrant children as citizens of the future. Immigrants rank high on the national priority list, and immigration receives a handsome budgetary allocation, which, theoretically, means the provision of optimal conditions for adjustment—an additional reason to study the Israeli experience.

Kovács and Cropley in their classic book *Immigrants and Society* (1975) distinguish between multicultural and monistic assimilation. Proponents of the latter regard cultural heterogeneity as negative and argue that a culture is socially healthy in direct proportion to its cultural homogeneity. Parallel cultural traditions within a single society are thought to be inimical to cultural unity and to be a source of perpetual strife unless they are eliminated as a result of compulsory, rapid, and total assimilation. This approach expects a swift and complete abandonment of the old ways and their replacement by the new—that are the only ones accepted. Thus alienation from the old is a precondition for assimilation. Given the massive volume of immigration and the emphasis on nation building, the monistic assimilationist orientation accurately describes the prevailing attitudes toward immigrants in Israel during the first 2 decades of independent statehood. This is the atmosphere that dominated teacher training, as I have shown in the previous chapter. Following that pioneering era and in reaction to increasing criticism (Ben-Rafael, 1982; Kahane, 1986; Smooha, 1978), a more pluralistic integrationist approach has been advocated. But as we learn from the previous chapter, reality and advocacy went their separate ways.

As shown in chapter two in both the case of the Russians and the Transylvanians, the attitude to the new school and, by extension, to society generally is deeply influenced by the newcomers' school experiences in their countries of origin. This finding places heavy responsibility on the educational system of the receiving society. Operationally, it means that the process of educational adaptation does not begin with the immigrant students' arrival at their new school and the preparation of a few special programs but stretches back into the past, to an understanding of the students' cultural-educational history. Although immigration constitutes a break in the life of individuals and their families, I found that when the educational services of the receiving country were more attuned to a continuum than to a breach orientation, the chances for a smooth transition and a thorough adjustment were enhanced.

Minimizing discontinuity between the school and home cultures as a precondition for successful school performance is a focal issue in educational anthropology. Discontinuity is an important factor in the case of immigrant children. The act of immigration constitutes a disruption, separation from friends and familiar surroundings. The immigrant family is often exposed to shattering transformation. Parents' career changes upset the equilibrium of family relationships and heads of families frequently experience loss of power. New demands are placed on children and adolescents to mediate between family and officialdom because young people are usually the first to gain mastery of the new language. All this affects the child's position in the changing family power structure. The emotional burden of prematurely imposed responsibility is heavy (Toren, 2003). The family loses effectiveness in performing its main social function, that of providing a haven of security for its members who then become more exposed and vulnerable. This discontinuity can only be met successfully by an active involvement of parents in the process of their children's school integration. As they represent the first encounter with a large normative institution of the new society and take place at a stage when there is little understanding of the wider social context, school practices are frequently perceived as arbitrary. To avoid mutual misunderstandings that generate discontent and mistrust, it is the schools' responsibility to engage in intensive informal family education to build effective channels of communication.

The five schools in the present sample took this broad acculturative role with varying degrees of seriousness. I closely examined educational philosophy, style of management, staff-staff, staff-student, student-student, and school-community relations, and different definitions of who is considered a new immigrant and for how long. Regarding the point when one is thought to be successfully integrated, these schools fall into two main clusters, yielding two composite models of educational treatment of NIS. I refer to the first as assimilationist or model A and the second as integrationist or model B.

An ethnological reporting style is used, that is interpretive and theory based rather than purely descriptive (Wolcott, 1975). The cultural milieux of the schools are analyzed with the following question in mind: What constitutes an optimal ecology for long-term adaptation of NIS? The practices in model A are not considered to be viable alternatives to those in model B, and the study attempts to demonstrate why this is so. Model B is guided by culturally informed, humane principles; model A defies the basic anthropological tenet of cultural relativism, which is at the core of genuine pluralism and a holistic approach to culturally different students. However, at the stage of data collection, no preexisting bias toward any school practice can be reported. A 3-month period of unfocused observation in all five sites preceded the more focused study of the models outlined above (Flick, 2006; Wolcott, 1999). There was no intention to "test" either model A or model B positions.

MODEL A SITES

I begin at Seaport because it houses three out of the five schools studied and two of the three schools that make up model A. Seaport is a relatively new, densely populated suburb of Northern City, mainly inhabited by immigrants. Its absorption center provides temporary housing facilities, as well as guidance and counseling services, for recent arrivals (adults) who participate in full-time language study programs. Seaview, which serves these NIS, is a new elementary school in the vicinity of the absorption center. The majority of the school population is made up of the children of veteran Israeli young couples attracted to the neighborhood by its inexpensive, yet high-quality, new housing project. According to the principal, these parents' educational level is high and they are active partners in the life of the school.

A discrepancy between school philosophy, expressed by the principal in the interviews and observed practice recorded during participant observation, was noted. Statements such as "the veteran population is making efforts to absorb the new immigrants" were made in the interviews with the principal. However, I observed no evidence of such activity taking place in school nor did the staff or students mention it. The principal also maintained that "during the last years absorption of new immigrants has become an established tradition." In this same vein he added that Seaview is not just another school whose role it is to teach youngsters." Instead, the school's philosophy is that "the institution should instill in the students a sense of belonging to the wider community and the nation at large." Yet, I found no reflection of this concern in either the activities or the material culture of the school. NIS did not play an active role in festivities observed during the year, not even as choir members, although many could sing well and had previous experience. During the communal Passover meal held with the parents, there was no mention of new families—

originating from the FSU —for some of whom this Biblical holiday of liberation had literal meaning.

The school was involved in several community projects and the principal took pride in them. The students regularly visited the sick and elderly in two hospitals, and they "adopted" the soldiers of a certain army unit with whom they exchanged visits and letters. The school took part in fund raising campaigns for various causes. I observed no active recruitment of NIS to participate in these activities nor any activity conducted for the benefit of NIS or their families living in the absorption center near the school.

The principal believed in an "egalitarian approach" toward all students. "The sooner the new immigrants become regular students the better." He did not know these children or their parents personally. "For this purpose there are excellent teachers in whom I confide with closed eyes. These teachers enjoy full autonomy and turn to me only in case of need." But funds from the Ministry of Education for these students were channeled through the principal who had no firsthand knowledge of their needs.

Following the principal's recommendations, I met the *Ulpan* teachers who were "really in charge." The *Ulpan* class, serving the first three grades (6–9 age group), was a tiny double-purpose room also serving as the infirmary. The teacher of the *Ulpan* class stated, "The children here are wrapped in cotton wool, get extra special treatment" in matters that were not related to the *Ulpan*, that is, were not intrinsically part of language learning. The teacher complained about her work load. She served as the "natural address" for requests and queries from parents, children, and workers in the absorption center. She did not question who should be doing this job or whether it needed to be done, but her message was unmistakable—for her the amount of work was excessive.

The *Ulpan* teachers were indeed autonomous decision makers, There were two teachers—one for the lower (ages 6–9) and one for the upper grades (ages 9–12). Both felt the burden of responsibility was too heavy and incommensurate with the scant, nonsystematic on-the-job preparation they had received. The principal referred to his policy of noninterference as a vote of confidence in the teachers, who, in turn, interpreted it as lack of interest and a reflection of the low priority given their work by the administrator. They also believed that children should spend a relatively short time in the *Ulpan* class and join the regular classes as early as possible. These teachers felt trapped between their desire to help people in need and the organization's lack of concern for their efforts. The *Ulpan* teachers, who were not part of the school's full-time staff, felt overburdened and marginal and did not, or could not, spare the time for coordination with the rest of the staff. Consequently, the latter considered the *Ulpan* a waste of time. All parties involved treated the need for *Ulpan* classes as temporary—hence not worth institutionalization or formal division of roles. The question of how effective the *Ulpan* could be under these circumstances was not tackled, and no one seemed aware that disorganization was lengthening the process considerably.

The 6-months period ordinarily devoted to language learning was divided into two trimester units. During the first trimester, the NIS spent their time exclusively in the *Ulpan*, concentrating on language and general orientation skills. During the second trimester, partial integration into the *Kitot em* (home rooms) took place for some Hebrew and all science classes. *Kitat em* (*Kitot* for plural)—literally mother class or home room with a head teacher *(Mechanech)*— was the basic educational structural unit in which most subjects were studied. Individual students or groups branched out from the *Kitot em* for specific subject matter interests. The term *Kitat em* was in common usage for both elementary and high school grades. Potentially more appropriate for the relatively intimate framework of the elementary classroom, the "mother" metaphor was hardly applicable in the large anonymous setting of the high school. Actually, from the view point of the NIS in both elementary and high school contexts, its usage is ironic as it refers to the often hostile, culturally heterogeneous larger classroom, as I have shown in chapters 1 and 2. In the *Ulpan* students received tutorial help with the specialized vocabulary of the various subjects. For the exams taken in the *Ulpan* class the students did not receive grades. Joining the *Kitot em* was regarded as an act of normalization. The *Ulpan* was generally viewed by the regular teachers as a rite of passage enabling immigrants to become real students and get report cards like the others.

The perspective of the NIS at Seaview was different. Some of the older students felt the time spent in the *Ulpan* was too short because they could not fully follow the lessons in the *Kitot em*. A recurring complaint was: "In Russia I was a top student. Here I don't understand what the teacher is saying. I can't do my homework without assistance, so my parents keep telling me I am not trying hard enough."

In spite of official statements to the contrary, the observed lack of organization resulted in inefficient treatment of NIS in this school. This view was reinforced by a unanimous sense of frustration shared by all those individuals who were directly involved—regular teachers, *Ulpan* teachers and, most of all, the NIS and their families.

Rivers is the only high school in Seaport. It offers a special program for NIS preparing them for the matriculation examinations as do the other two high schools in the sample. As indicated in chapter one, in these programs, students enjoy certain privileges. They can choose to take oral exams in the Hebrew subjects, social studies, and humanities, administered by examiners who speak their native languages. By examinations in the language and literature of their native tongue students can obtain second-language credits. The Rivers buildings stretch over a large area and the atmosphere inside the school is dominated by the grey color of the concrete. The yard is bleak and the corridors are dark and undecorated.

In our first conversation, the principal stated that all his efforts were concentrated on the educational program. Ecological awareness and concern for quality of life for students and staff were not considered part of the program. The principal complained about the problems of serving a transient population. For lack of sufficient job opportunities, many of the new immigrants arriving in Seaport stayed there only temporarily. Representing the students' interests, school officials often attempted to convince parents to give children the chance to complete their high school education before moving. Otherwise, these students tended to drop out of the system altogether. There was no mention of any initiative taken by the school administration to provide alternative living arrangements in Seaport for those students who wished to stay behind without their families in order to complete their studies at Rivers. In effect, no ongoing school-community involvement was documented.

The principal at Rivers also handled NIS through delegated authority rather than in person. A coordinator was in charge of the program. There were two *Ulpan* classes whose teachers were open and cooperative. Teacher-student relations were warm, and a genuine learning atmosphere prevailed in the classes. The coordinator, however, was particularly defensive, even suspicious, in her attitude to research in general. A veteran immigrant from the Former Soviet Union (FSU), her attitude might have been influenced by negative experiences in prior attempts to utilize research information. Her attempts to control investigative activities—for instance, by insisting on obtaining her permission to interview students and parents in their homes after they had consented to cooperate—resulted in a decision to withdraw from this setting before the completion of the study. All this occurred despite preparatory discussion with school officials about research plans. I would have liked to learn more about the dynamics of this positive learning experience characterized by informal relationships between teachers and students with the latter encouraged to keep a collective journal to record their feelings. On the whole, learning was subject-matter and goal oriented with success on the matriculation exams in view.

The coordinator discouraged *Ulpan* teachers from dealing directly with families, defining the classroom as their only scope of activity. Students' adjustment-related problems were defined as personal and were declared outside of the school's radius of interest. Thus the principal's claim regarding the efforts made to keep students in school remained unvalidated. Nor did I find out how the transition from the *Ulpan* class to the *Kitot em* occurred. Here, too, 6 months was considered the ideal amount of time to be spent in that setting.

Newtown, a northern development town with a predominant new immigrant population, is a planned community based on high-technology industries designed to absorb educated and skilled workers. Its environmental conception and landscaping make it attractive to the new immigrants who arrive there. Unlike Seaport, most newcomers make Newtown their permanent residence.

Newtown High is a large comprehensive school that also offers a special program for NIS. Like Seaport and Rivers the school stresses "fast absorption"—that is, a short *Ulpan* period and a philosophy of "egalitarian treatment" of NIS. Because of the general awareness of cultural diversity in a town whose very existence depends on it, one would expect the only high school in the community to be sensitive to the specific needs of NIS.

Instead, the principal summed up the school philosophy in the following terms: "NIS are an integral part of a *Kitat em* and expected to take part in social activities like the rest of our students." The message seems to be that the school is a complex organization with various streams—vocational, academic, college preparatory—and the staff's main objective is to distribute the students among these various slots. The perception of a homogeneous student body—that is, minimum attention to individual differences—dominates, and the school employs a subject-matter and organizational-framework-oriented approach. A focus on the cultural differences of NIS would have required to further partition the student population. The question that immediately arose was to what extent should a community in a state of constant flux, receiving new immigrants from different cultural and educational backgrounds, maintain such a rigid structure instead of a more flexible, individualized program. The rhetoric of equality minimized the problem of appropriate educational programs for these students.

I studied the *Ulpan* classes as the organizational frameworks that handle the NIS, examining their functions to serve the client population, to convey to them a sense of equality in attitudes, allocation of resources, and maximization of their future opportunities. There were three such special frameworks in the school, two at the junior high and one at the senior high level, the latter being a matriculation-exam-preparatory class. The physical location of the *Ulpan* classes provided the first negative finding. *Ulpan* I (for the junior high students) was located in an isolated underground air raid shelter with no windows, a heavy iron door, and artificial illumination. In spite of the austere surroundings, Vered, the teacher, attempted to create an intimate atmosphere. She treated the students as individuals and made a point of spending time with each of them separately. (I will have more to say about Vered's role below.)

The more advanced junior high NIS went on to *Ulpan* II, located in a warehouse-turned-classroom in the school yard facing the basketball court. The high noise level made concentration in class difficult. The long, narrow shape of the room was not suited to its function. The teacher, whose desk was in the center, could barely make eye contact with the students sitting at the far ends of the room. Eager students sat near the teacher, and rowdy ones chose the edges of the room where they got only occasional negative attention. The teacher assigned to this *Ulpan* class took maternity leave in the middle of the year. Her replacement was a novice with no experience working with NIS. She appeared to be a strict disciplinarian with little interest in the students' cultural background and problems. Some complained about having had three different *Ulpan* teachers during their first year in the new country and school.

As part of the philosophy of assimilation into the mainstream, the *Ulpan* was designed as a purposive learning environment. It was not intended to meet the students' social needs. Indeed, little out-of-school social interaction was noted. The students wandered between the *Kitot em* and the *Ulpan*, frustrated and alienated, not really part of either.

The school counselor was not up-to-date on the unique problems of recent immigrants. Her theory was, "If there were problems I would have heard." I learned that here, too, there was a special social coordinator for NIS, but the designated person had neither the skills nor the initiative to do outreach work. Consequently, as in Rivers, only problems brought up by parents received attention.

The teacher of *Ulpan* I, Vered, became the person most cognizant of the students' problems. As she was a veteran teacher, experienced in working with adult new immigrants, Vered responded wholeheartedly to this challenge. The children expressed deep satisfaction with her attitude toward them. She carried on her activity despite receiving no organizational endorsement. As in Seaport and Rivers, Vered was not part of the regular school staff. But since she considered work with NIS as part of her personal mission, and her professional identity was anchored in being an established *Ulpan* teacher for adults, she was less dependent on organizational confirmation. I observed the same pattern emerging in each locale: the *Ulpan* and the *Ulpan* teacher were not regarded as an integral part of the school culture.

The only framework for NIS in this school, one that inadvertently met both the students' social and scholastic needs, was the special matriculation-exam-preparatory program for the upper grades. Here the students spent most of their time together, rather than shuttling back and forth between the *Ulpan* and the regular classes. Meaningful relations with their teachers were formed and they achieved a sense of belonging. The fulfillment of social needs enhanced scholastic achievement. This "success," however, was the by-product of chance occurrence rather than planned policy. Its real source went unnoticed by the school administration.

MODEL B SITES

Pioneers Elementary School and Lighthouse High School represent the integrationist approach to immigrant students, referred to as model B. Pioneers is situated in the northern section of Seaport near the old, no longer active, absorption center. The area is neglected, the outward appearance of the houses is dilapidated. Garbage-filled empty lots are a common sight. Pioneers was built in the 80s. Its well-kept one-story building is surrounded by a flourishing garden divided into small labeled plots. The school's greenery stands in sharp contrast to its surrounding neighborhood.

The principal told me that the school had, for a time, been an object of vandalism, a target for the inhabitants' antiestablishment feelings. Slowly, however, the situation changed. Through a series of community-oriented projects geared to involving parents as well as other citizen groups, antagonism gradually gave way to active support.

The material culture of the school was the best indication of the importance accorded the subject of immigration and cultural variety. A huge diagram on the central wall displayed the students' countries of origin. Next to each label was the flag and a doll in the national costume. The issue of immigrants and immigration was a central project for the school. Teachers received special training through a series of lectures by various professionals, representatives of local services, and members of different ethnic groups. Informative fliers were prepared and distributed to students and parents. Media instruction included written sources, audiovisual materials, visits to the ethnological museum, and live accounts by parents and grandparents. The culmination of the project was a meticulously organized exhibition set up by joint teams of teachers, students, and parents on the topic of *Kibbutz Galuiot* (ingathering of exiles) which stimulated much community interest.

NIS were assigned big brothers or sisters, veteran immigrants from their country of origin, who were prepared to assist them with the process of settling in. A gardening project allowed each interested parent-child team to receive a small plot for gardening in the school yard all year round. This project increased commitment to the upkeep of the school's physical plant. Parents volunteered to do various maintenance chores to help the school. The students themselves cleaned the building on a rotating basis. Money saved this way was devoted to nonacademic activities, for example, the purchase of special gym equipment, and so on. The classrooms and corridors were in excellent repair, filled with children's art work.

The principal personally welcomed the children (some 400) at the main entrance every morning. He knew their names and was aware of their individual problems. Unlike the principal at Seaview, he was directly involved in making decisions concerning the treatment of NIS.

A special team evaluated the educational achievements and Hebrew language proficiency of each student individually and made decisions about his or her program in coordination with the teacher of the future *Kitat em*. This long-range plan assured gradual transition to regular classes. The teacher of the *Kitat em* knew the exact schedule of her NIS and was able to locate them at all times. The teacher understood the importance of this preparatory program.

The *Ulpan* class was permanently based on the main floor in a special room adapted to small group and individual learning and alongside the rest of the classes. The *Ulpan* teachers made home calls on a regular basis. There was no coordinator as in the other schools. The *Ulpan* teacher performed this task and handled further school-related problems the family might encounter. She explained the various school activities to parents and encouraged them to take part. Nonschool-related problems were referred to the proper services. The *Ulpan* teacher was an informal support for the entire family. The *Ulpan* group was small, and the teacher could afford the time for a holistic treatment of the new immigrant child in his or her family context.

Once the *Ulpan* was completed, and students were in the *Kitat em*, they were still entitled to tutorial help. The big sister or brother arrangement continued officially for a year and often produced lasting friendships. Immigrant students and their heritages were welcome in the school. Not only were their heritages tolerated but they were considered a source of enrichment for everyone. In this climate, even the most recent arrivals were able to take an active part in all school celebrations.

Lighthouse High School is located in Northern City on an elevation overlooking the Mediterranean, which provides a scenic view from each classroom window. The school is housed in a new building designed with optimal concern for ecological suitability. It is surrounded by lawns where students are seen relaxing and chatting in small groups during breaks. It is colorfully painted inside, and the landscaping and view create a pleasant learning environment. The school is dedicated to the education of a pluralistic student population including Bahai and Druze youngsters, in addition to new immigrants. Some students, whose families live out of town, travel as far as 100 km each way daily to attend this school. Others live in university dormitories by special arrangement.

The principal states the school's philosophy as follows.

> The school took on the integration of immigrants as one of its major projects because of the potential for mutuality it involves. It educates the Israeli students to actively cope with the pluralism the NIS bring to school. At the same time it offers the newcomers the opportunity to adjust to their environment in a receptive atmosphere.

Lighthouse used liberal rules and interpretations concerning time and age limits to enable a maximum number of NIS to enjoy their special services. To this end, the school offered a special program to young people beyond high school in the 18–24 age bracket. The program provided these youth with one "last chance" to obtain a matriculation certificate, a requirement for higher education. Students were housed in university dormitories through the dedicated intervention of the regional superintendent for NIS affairs, who took personal care of them. They all arrived in Israel without families and thus had no primary support network. The efficient cooperation between the superintendent and the school's principal established optimal conditions for these young adults. Since they were full-time students, the school subsidized their travel expenses as well as other basic necessities. Although some difficulties with the integration of this group into a regular high school could have been anticipated, no such problems arose. These students were allowed to keep to themselves.

There was no intervention to expedite the process of mixing and mingling of the Israeli students and the newcomers. NIS were observed to chat loudly in their mother tongue during breaks. No stigma was attached to this practice and there was no pressure to speak Hebrew or to "act like an Israeli."

There were two additional *Ulpan* classes, one for the eleventh and one for the twelfth graders, with no set limits or prescribed norms as to how and when to join the *Kitot em*.[2] These students took the majority of subjects (except for the sciences) in the *Ulpan* classes as part of the special matriculation-preparatory program. During the class periods, individual students at times translated concepts into their mother tongue for the benefit of the other students. No teacher objections were noted. These classes were composed of confident youngsters bound by close intragroup relations, young people who felt accepted as they were. Ties with the rest of the students were gradually established through various informal extracurricular activities.

The *Ulpan* teachers were deeply committed, among the most highly regarded professionals in their areas of expertise. Hanna, the coordinator of the *Ulpan* program, who was also the Hebrew teacher, introduced herself to a newly arrived group of eleventh graders in the following way: "*Chevre* (informal for friends, fellows), I am your teacher, also your judge and policewoman, but I am a volunteer mother, too. You are welcome to take advantage of that." She achieved success with NIS by creating an atmosphere that allowed the youngsters to preserve their original values.

Other staff also contributed to the creation of this atmosphere. The' counselor spent a great deal of time working with this group. She knew everyone personally. Throughout the year of the study she ran weekly support groups where students could deal with their feelings of strangeness and loneliness in a new country, longings for friends left behind, differences in norms regarding adolescent behavior, communication problems with parents, and so on. These sessions provided recognition of their unique problems and support in handling them.

Neighborhood people were familiar with the school's activities, and school-community ties were strong. The students conducted various fund-raising campaigns, and the NIS participated in these activities. Neighborhood interest was also expressed in the willingness of many families to host new immigrant youngsters, particularly those without families in Israel, for weekends and holidays.

The humane, individualized approach toward NIS observed in this school, so clearly missing in the schools labeled model A, freed the youngsters to take an active part in volunteer activities. A 15-year-old new immigrant girl, 6 months in the country, "adopted" an autistic child and spent time with her regularly on a weekly basis. Since her needs were respected, she could turn to meet those of others in her new environment. In line with findings reported in chapter 2 whereby males could only relate to host culture peers on a power equal basis, NIS who were good mathematicians were asked for help by their Israeli classmates. NIS who were good athletes made friends with veteran youngsters on that common ground. They were thus given a chance to gradually ease into the receiving society on the basis of their inherent strengths rather than as needy, deficient members who needed to be reshaped first.

Table 6.1 summarizes the main features of the two prevailing approaches to new immigrant education.

IN CONCLUSION

In his seminal volume devoted to the study of identity, Fitzgerald (1974) makes a pertinent distinction between social and cultural identity. He maintains that social identity is situational and promotes the individual's behavioral adaptation to new contextual imperatives. Hence it facilitates change. Cultural identity, alternatively, transcends situational adjustments

Table 6.1. The Models

	Model A	Model B
Philosophy	- Equal attention to all students, new immigrants included; deproblematization of the status of NIS – narrowly defined as a group characterized by language deficiency considered a technical problem - Optimal time for adaptation: six months.	- Being a NIS is a legitimate status with its intrinsic problems which should be recognized, respected, and solved. - There is no prescribed time frame to terminate this period—no formal limits.
Style of management	- The principal delegates authority/responsibility to *Ulpan* teachers or coordinator for NIS affairs, does not know these students, their parents, and problems personally. The coordinator is not directly involved in teaching these students. Only handles problems brought by parents or individual NIS. - Same holds true for school counselor's approach. No outreach work. Only handles cases referred by the staff.	- The principal is involved in decision making concerning NIS. He knows these students and parents personally. Is interested in their nonschool related problems as well. Sees them as pertinent to their holistic educational treatment. - Either no coordinator function, or where it exists, the coordinator is actively teaching in the *Ulpan* setting, assisting students in defining as well as solving their problems.
Ulpan teachers' interpretation of the above and their position in the organization	- The *Ulpan* as a subsystem and their work in it are of secondary importance. Their work load is heavy as they are the natural address for parents' complaints, expected to solve urgent problems. - Yet, they are organizationally unrewarded. Their position is marginal. Not part of tenured staff	- The *Ulpan* is a well-integrated subsystem in the organization. Its self-contained educational program is conducted by senior members of the regular staff. - As work with NIS is considered particularly challenging, only highly regarded subject matter specialists are involved in it.

	- Frustrated and isolated, communication with the rest of the teachers is flawed, resulting in disorganization that further lowers their own status and that of the Ulpan altogether. These teachers receive irregular individual on-the-job training (consultation sessions) by outside specialists.	- These teachers work as a coordinated educational team, that initiates and conducts its own on-the-job training (occasionally consulting outside specialists).
Staff attitudes regarding the *Ulpan*	- The *Ulpan* is regarded as a source of disruption of daily routine in the *Kitat em*, a "necessary evil"—a period of preparation for NIS to assume regular membership in the school community, of little intrinsic scholastic or social value. Hence, the shorter the better. No report cards are given for subject matter learned in the *Ulpan*, denoting its transitional academic standing.	- The *Ulpan* is a regular school program with a well-defined schedule. All teachers are aware of and respect it.
	- Teachers pull out individual students from the *Ulpan* to participate in activities of social relevance in the *Kitat em* to help them feel as much a part of their "true" reference group as possible	- Individual NIS are welcome to join the regular classes for certain subject matter study, mostly the sciences, as soon as recommended by the *Ulpan* teacher/educational team.
	- Teachers do not encourage lasting friendships with other *Ulpan* members; they deemphasize its potential to serve as a primary reference group for NIS.	- Its status as a primary reference group for its members is recognized.
Social position of the NIS and the *Ulpan* as expressed by the material culture of the school	- The *Ulpan* is open for limited periods only, depending on the size of the NIS population at any given time.	- The *Ulpan* is permanently open regardless of the size of the NIS population in the school.
	- It is housed in makeshift special arrangements such as the nurse's room, an air raid shelter, a warehouse, etc., mostly isolated from the rest of the classrooms.	- It is housed in a regular classroom.

Table continues on next page.

Table 6.1. Continued

	Model A	Model B
	- The presence of culturally different students is not reflected in any of the classrooms or corridor mural displays.	- Vivid mural displays are devoted to the depiction of the cultures of origin of the NIS groups in the school.
NIS attitudes toward the *Ulpan* and overall school experience	- Some NIS would like to spend more time in the *Ulpan* as they feel the need for more thorough preparation before joining the *Kitot em* effectively. Others accept the verdict that "fast out" is a sign of success. Many interpret their lack of language proficiency for joining the regular program as their own fault/failure.	- NIS expressed overall satisfaction with their school experience and relationship with teachers and peers, both NIS and veteran Israelis. Saw the *Ulpan* as an efficient program that nevertheless allowed them to adapt at their own individual pace.
	- The students have no real reference group. They share a sense of social and scholastic liminality.	- The NIS' intensive participation in school festivities, extracurricular activities, and volunteer work in the community bear testimony to a high degree of integration in the school culture. The school counselor (in the high school) knows all NIS and holds weekly group support sessions with them to work on their specific problems.

and implies stability. As it is the source of larger group or ethnic identification, it contributes to the individual's continued behavioral coherence. When an assimilationist approach is adopted, as in model A schools, phenomena are treated on the superficial behavioral level of NIS' social identity. Accordingly, emphasis is on fast adaptation measured by academic achievement rather than on social and psychological adaptation, which are presumed to take place automatically in this normative framework. In model B, on the other hand, where an integrationist orientation is employed, the multilevel process of cultural adaptation of NIS, rather than concrete short-range outcomes, is the central focus. A concerted effort is made to cause the least possible damage to students' cultural identities.

The complete disregard of the immigrant peer group through a negation of the *Ulpan's* social functions impedes both educational and social adaptation in model A. Since they recognize only immigrant students' difficulties that stem from a lack of language proficiency, these schools deny their wider societal responsibility as primary agents of acculturation. This attitude deepens the schism in the new immigrant child's life and further enhances the existential perception of immigration as a traumatic experience. A sense of both social and scholastic liminality is fostered. In rites-of-passage theory, liminality is defined as the stage of transition to the new, following that of separation from former group or state, and is characterized by insecurity and anxiety (Turner, 1970).

As earlier reiterated, assimilation or "monistic assimilation" in an educational context is usually advocated on ideological grounds—to stress national unity, particularly in the framework of nation building (Ben-Shalom & Horenczyk, 2004; Shuval, 1998) and on economic grounds, as it offers a rationale for applying a uniform, hence more cost efficient approach to teacher training and curriculum development. As indicated earlier, these gains are short-lived. Problems stemming from the NIS' cultural liminality are swept under the rug only to be polarized later and more difficult to handle because of accumulated bitterness.

In model B programs a continuum is fostered. The trauma of sudden cultural change with its ensuing disorientation is paralyzing. Only by reestablishing a sense of continuity can the individual resume efficient functioning in the new environment. As I have demonstrated, these schools attempt to provide close to optimal conditions for this process to occur.

Chances for successful educational integration could be further enhanced by a systematic anthropological study of the school cultures in the NIS' countries of origin. As I have shown in chapter one, information on school climates, norms, disciplinary practices, teaching-learning styles, curricular issues, school-parent relations, parental perceptions about what constitutes a good school, canons for teacher evaluation, attitudes toward regular attendance—would provide educators a broader understanding of the source and nature of the difficulties NIS and their families encounter. Through such insight, the host schools can improve their own effectiveness in actively helping them overcome some of their more vexing problems.

This study offers an in vivo demonstration of how assimilationist versus integrationist orientations are translated into actual educational practice and how they are experienced by NIS, their parents, and also the school personnel involved. The description of the settings is rounded to impart an overall view of everyday life in these schools. The way they tackle this particular issue is not to be divorced from the totality of the school environment within which it is embedded. The necessity of taking such a contextualized approach to gain a thorough understanding of the problems and to facilitate social and scholastic adjustment is, indeed, an important part of its message.

The organizational cultures of schools have many common features. The detailed idiographic portrayal of the settings from which these operational-level, middle-range generalizations have been derived, allows discerning readers to critically assess the degree of applicability of these findings to their reality, thereby making cautious cross-setting and even cross-cultural borrowing feasible. The findings of the study—as they pertain to optimal conditions for long-range cross-cultural adaptation of NIS —can be summarized in the following generalizations.

This research indicates that a positive school experience in a receiving society requires that the school authorities accept the NIS' problems as legitimate. The concerns of these students must not be dismissed as the "gripes" one has to expect. That is, the acceptance of problems lessens their fears. Equally useful is refraining from stating limits to the time during which one can remain in NIS status. This helps students to relax and give attention to learning the host language and to fulfilling other requirements in the course of study. As a complement to these efforts at lessening NIS' apprehensiveness, these findings clearly suggest that smooth adjustment in school—and in society generally—calls for a maximum degree of parental involvement. It is not difficult to get involvement in extracurricular activities such as cultural displays, festivals, and the maintenance of the school and school grounds. Every effort should be made to give expression to the varied cultural heritages represented by the backgrounds of the NIS. This attention signals a respect for their cultural background—essential for building trust. In the preparation of exhibits, as well as other cultural demonstrations, communication with peers from the receiving society is furthered on a more egalitarian basis.

Special programs for NIS must be central in the organizational structure of the school. The programs must be coordinated with the rest of the organization and curriculum. If they are, one can expect the educational experience of these students to be enhanced. While organizational centrality is essential, it is not a substitute for the direct involvement of school personnel. This is what lessens the chances for the NIS to feel alienated and marginal. Harm to cultural identity can and should be minimized. Along with minimizing harm to these youngsters' senses of cultural identity, school personnel must adopt an approach that is always individualized, that introduces expectations gradually, and that centers attention on subject matter. This will help achieve and maintain positive self-evaluation.

As a final note, I urge recognition for the program devised for the NIS as a primary reference group. Such recognition is likely to improve both scholastic achievement and long-term positive attitudes toward the receiving society. As the receiving society demonstrates increasing tolerance toward individual as well as cultural differences, many of the problems outlined here will be effectively solved. These seem to be preconditional steps for creating the conditions that would gradually lead to rapprochement and effective collaboration between newcomers and locals—a sine qua non for enhancing the global fitness of today's youth.

NOTES

1. I am indebted to Aharon Borstein, regional superintendent for New Immigrant Student Affairs, Ministry of Education, for introductions at the research sites and to Malka Shabtay for assistance in coordinating the data collection.
2. In this school the junior high level *Ulpan* program was not studied as it was very small and was just beginning a new session.

CHAPTER 7

AN ANTHROPOLOGICAL ANSWER

The Teacher-as-Ethnographer Model

The previous two chapters prepared us for the realization that in order to cope with immigrant students effectually and help them maximize their potential, a reconceptualization of multicultural teacher training is necessary. To achieve this teachers have to learn how to create classroom cultures that allow or, better, encourage their youngsters to treat their heritage as a source of continuous inspiration and enrichment rather than discard it as irrelevant. Only in such a climate can intercultural cooperation grow.

From the comparative ethnographic study described in chapter 6 in which I explored different styles of approaching immigrant education in Israeli schools, I developed a set of generalizable conditions for optimizing the social and academic functioning of immigrant students in the schools of their receiving societies (see pp. 133–135). Here I am going to present an anthropological action model for teacher training, operationalized as an intervention program I call "The Teacher-as-Ethnographer," which is based on these principles. Originally designed as an in-service training program, in order to provide immediate answers to urgent needs, the action model is adaptable to preservice use, as well.

Immigrant Youth Who Excel: Globalization's Uncelebrated Heroes, pp. 137–150
Copyright © 2008 by Information Age Publishing
All rights of reproduction in any form reserved.

Its potential for cross-cultural and cross-training level applicability is examined.

The illustrative material is drawn from the context of working with New immigrant students (NIS), specifically Russian immigrants in Israel. Being a new immigrant is interpreted in this volume as a condition in which the individual experiences an acute form of cultural difference. Referring to the American context, some writers (Suárez-Orozco, 1989; Gibson & Ogbu, 1991) distinguish between the motivational orientation of immigrant students, which they call "voluntary" minorities, and students belonging to nonimmigrant groups, labeled "involuntary" or "caste-like" minorities. Contrary to the first category's favorable predisposition, the latter are assumed to develop a stance of resistance toward schools and educational achievement, resulting from a multigenerational experience of denial of opportunities by the dominant society. The above distinction between patterns of student response notwithstanding, this chapter proposes a training model for the preparation of multiculturally competent school staff (including teachers, counsellors. administrators, etc.) able to diagnose and cater to the needs of all students from culturally diverse backgrounds (Eldering, 1996). As used here, this term covers immigrant as well as nonimmigrant ethnic and religious minority youngsters.

DESCRIPTION OF THE PROGRAM

I was aided in conducting this intervention, which took place in Upper Hilltown, by three graduate research assistants from the University of Haifa, School of Education.[1] Since their assistance was mostly technical, I continue to use first person narration. Site selection was based on the fact that this community received the highest percentage of new immigrants during the 1990s, as mentioned in chapter one. Participants included educators from all levels of the local system: elementary, junior high and high schools. In addition to teachers—school psychologists, counselors, social workers, representatives of informal educational organizations, and top level administrative staff also took part. The experimental program comprised of lectures, workshops, school visits and on-site individual and group consultation sessions. It was concentrated to one 8-hour day weekly, and spanned the entire school year.

The program had three parts: During the first part, which I named: "The Teacher-as-Anthropologist," concepts derived from anthropological theory were introduced to allow a deeper understanding of various adaptation problems of new immigrants. The second part, which I titled "The Teacher-as-Ethnographer" (TAE)[2] concentrated on ethnographic methods for data collection and analysis. Using the theoretical material as a base, trainees experimented with these techniques and applied them to real-life situations. The third and last part was devoted to the design, implementation and writing up of individual or group research projects on topics chosen and defined by the participants. Familiarized with the ethnographic research sequence, they came to recognize its potential to transform intuitive action into systematic knowledge.

By the end of the intervention these educators exhibited abilities to analyze in holistic cultural terms problems they had previously perceived in the narrow context of the school. Organization-based as opposed to individual participation enhanced the formation of support groups and 'think teams' which facilitated continued discussion, and application of the new concepts and skills. The community-wide, interdisciplinary nature of the training program demonstrated the efficacy of such a framework for problem solving in general.

Creating a positive predisposition for immigrant youths to function effectively in an educational system different from the one in their country of origin is indispensable for successful work with these students. This can be only achieved by acknowledging the intrinsic importance of NIS' social adaptation—as in model B schools described in the previous chapter—rather than focusing exclusively on academic achievement, as in model A schools portrayed in that same chapter. As I have reiterated, when school staffs define their mandate narrowly, as one of imparting knowledge, they do not recognize the organization's acculturative role. Social adaptation depends on a combination of local factors which means that uniform materials cannot be relied upon. Ignoring regional differences that may exist in a country of origin, such as between immigrants from the European and Asian parts of the Former Societ Union (FSU), or immigrants to France from the northern or southern parts of the Magreb countries; between urbanites or rural populations, or those stemming from parents' level of education, to name only a few examples, reinforces stereotypes towards immigrant and minority students (Ngo, 2006). In view of this, the importance of ethnographic skills for teachers working with multicultural populations becomes all the more apparent. Equipped to study and better understand the unique needs of their students, these educators will be able to develop culture appropriate teaching methods and curriculum content.

This intervention program aimed at bringing about change on the level of participants' attitudes and premised to entail long range behavioral transformation. At the beginning, trainees were at a loss for 'quick fixes'. The volume of NIS flocking into their classes on a daily basis was overwhelming, sweeping away all certitude about "proper" class management (Freeman, Brookhart, & Loadman, 1999; Leiding, 2007). However, at the end of the intervention these same teachers maintained they were no longer afraid of change. Instead, they reported to have acquired an empowering sense of competence to handle new situations.

THE TEACHER-AS-ANTHROPOLOGIST

The first part of the program introduced participants to anthropological concepts. Whenever possible a problem-based approach was adopted in the meetings. Group discussions were used to relate these concepts to classroom or school situations that would best illustrate them. During the weekly visits and consultation sessions, educators had further opportunities to apply concepts, thereby reframing their current interactions with NIS. While some of this material is presented here in detailed contextualized format to demonstrate actual application, other concepts, and their use is only briefly mentioned.

In one instance value judgments held by participants were identified and incorporated into the program. Participants were overheard complaining to each other that many of the NIS had difficulties concentrating, seemed unmotivated and did not prepare their assignments regularly. One teacher added that this was in opposition to all she had heard about "kids from Russia, who were supposed to be disciplined and conscientious students." This piece of conversation was used as the starting point for the next meeting to discuss expressions of NIS' malfunctioning in school, as part of the larger problem of immigrant family dysfunctionality, discussed in chapter 6. To do this, I introduced ecological, materialist, and cognitive definitions of culture (see Kaplan & Manners, 1972; Kottak, 2002; Spradley, 1980) as they apply to immigrant families.

From an ecological standpoint, culture was defined as an adaptive mechanism a population develops to adjust to its environment; a process-oriented materialist approach singles out the subsistence means of a population, that is, how it makes a living: by hunting and gathering, intensive or extensive agriculture, industrial means, and so forth—as part of its ecological adaptation.

Concentrating on the family as the unit of analysis, it was demonstrated in the program how such adaptive mechanisms lose a great deal of their viability in the context of migration. As a result, members of immigrant families experience extreme imbalance and incongruity with their new surroundings. This explanation helped participants grasp the high incidence of family disintegration and emotional problems, as well as the interconnectedness of these phenomena. Immigrant children bring along to school the problems of a family struggling with the results of cultural uprootedness. The time perception of people in a state of crisis is focused on the present. The intensity of their problems impinges upon their ability to develop a future orientation. Understanding how these out-of-school, family-system level circumstances affect in-school functioning, will improve teachers' abilities to reassess their expectations. Cross-disciplinary cooperation between educators and other providers of human services in the school and in the community can help the entire family find a way out of its existential impasse.

I presented another materialist approach to culture which emphasized artifacts a group produces. In addition to such staples of folk art as weaving. embroidery and pottery, modern electronic technology (such as videotape recordings) affords the preservation and presentation of more abstract aspects of culture such as music, dancing, live storytelling or even the reproduction of a whole event. For groups of immigrants this can serve as an important vehicle for combating negative stereotypes created in the course of initial encounters with institutions and representatives of the host society. Portraying various aspects of their tradition in school-organized folk events and performances that involve the families, offers an opportunity to improve intercultural communication, as demonstrated in chapter 6. The message thus transmitted to NIS is one of openness and acceptance of their heritage, thereby establishing a basis for mutual respect. This, in turn, encourages a positive predisposition for exploring or even adopting aspects of the host culture relevant to NIS

From a cognitive perspective, following Spradley's (1980) classical definition, culture can be envisioned as a set of rules, norms and values, a language, a grammar or a map to follow. In his words: "the acquired knowledge people use to interpret experience and generate behavior" (p. 6). This view helps clarify why any new culture becomes accessible to people who were not born into it only as a system of ideas they have to learn. This further highlights the acculturative role of the formal educational system and particularly that of the teachers. The participants realize that while the previous three definitions link the notion of culture to a territory, this one locates it in people's heads. In other words, this approach makes knowledge—the stuff of culture, and a group of people with such shared knowledge—a culture in the cognitive sense. This enables us to conceive of professional groups (e.g., physicians, lawyers, teachers), of organizations and their subsystems, such as hospitals, schools, classrooms or even families—as cultural units. They all have exclusive knowledge, overt and covert symbols, a unique structure, and rules for new members to join. A cultural study of small groups justifies the application of anthropological theory in their analysis.

This line of reasoning led participants to conclude that membership in such cognitive cultures entails the assumption of several identities. For example, adults may have a professional identity, a political identity and a family identity. Youngsters may have a classroom cultural identity, a peer group identity or a sports and recreation affiliated identity. One's ability to simultaneously handle these sometimes conflicting cultural memberships and identities becomes a measure of one's adaptation in complex modern societies.

These educators gained a new perspective on the predicament of new immigrant children who are often expected to operate in cognitive contexts with highly discrepant demands. The home and the school, peer group affiliations, different intraschool settings that have already been introduced in previous chapters such as the *Ulpan* and the *Kitot Em* are only a few. Perceiving the classroom as a culture helped participants improve their communication with new immigrant students. Furthermore, it allowed them to identify the various cognitive subcultures among their students, to recognize the composition of natural groups during breaks, friendship networks in youth groups, extracurricular activities, sports groups, and so forth, thereby better understanding the sociometric position of each student. This information can be used to form more effective learning groups.

Another conceptual tool trainees reported to have found applicable was an observation guide I developed based on Margaret Mead's (n.d.) renowned ethnographic film *Four Families*," in which she comparatively studied child-rearing practices and attitudes in an East-Indian, French, Japanese and Canadian family. The observation guide called the attention of the "teacher-ethnographer" to: background information on the observed family (urban or rural, occupation, income, education of parents) age, sex, and number of children; male and female roles in income earning; in child rearing; interaction between fathers and their children of different ages (focus on specific acts and activities); mothers' interactions with children (list of acts and activities); amount of time spent on child rearing chores, time of the day, verbal and nonverbal communication between parents (separately) and children of various ages; disciplining methods used; family role distribution (during meals, for example); toys and games; material culture of the household; use of space by various family members, and so forth. Items can be added or substituted for. To study an extended or multigenerational family other items will be relevant.

The systematic application of such an observation guide enabled participants to comparatively study child-rearing in their own family, other families from a similar ethno-socioeconomic background, and various immigrant families through comparable parameters. Observation was supplemented by interviews with family members, the use of photographs to elicit information on details of the material culture.

A better appreciation of the importance of primary socialization patterns facilitates the adaptation of school activities to harmonize with home cultures—a necessary condition for students' optimal functioning.

The sensitization of TAEs to the influence of their own home culture on their attitudes is likely to sharpen these practitioners' awareness to personal biases (Otoya-Knapp, 2005), resulting in improved cross-cultural competence.

Using Margaret Mead's ageless book *Culture and Commitment: The Study of the Generation Gap* (1970) as a frame of reference, I designed an additional analytic device for the participants' use. In this book Mead distinguishes among styles of cross-generational culture transmission in societies undergoing varying degrees of change. Highly conservative traditional ones, such as tribal societies or religious sects, she labels as "post-figurative." Societies undergoing moderate change are called "co-figurative" and rapidly changing societies— "pre-figurative." People from post-figurative societies turn to the past to select their model for living and transmit their culture unidirectionally from elders, as experts, to the young, whose role is limited to absorbing the tradition. In co-figurative cultures there is intergenerational exchange in culture transmitting functions, with a division according to spheres of knowledge: tradition represented by elders and the techno-economic domain, by the young. Pre-figurative refers to an emergent culture, where the accelerated pace of change cuts across intergenerational dividing lines.

Expanding on Mead's (1970) conceptualization, I devised the following model presented in Table 7.1 to help participants understand processes that immigrant or minority groups might encounter in the course of their interactions within a complex, culturally heterogeneous society. Such items as the role of schools, the role of learners and learning styles, participants were instructed to extrapolate from the above-mentioned scenarios, as an exercise in heuristic thinking. Under the post-figurative heading I also included groups interested in the preservation of a certain blueprint for social life based on a political ideology—such as in a Communist regime, relevant for working with immigrant students from the

Table 7.1. Rate of Social Change and Style of Cross-Generational Culture Transmission

Societies	The Knowledge Deemed Important To Transmit	Optimal Cultural Transmitters	The Status of Cultural Transmitters	The Role of the Learners and Style of Learning	The Role and Importance of Schools
Post-figurative					
Co-figurative					
Pre-figurative					

FSU. In such a milieu, learners are also expected to model, listen, and memorize.

As they fill in the table, participants realize that in traditional societies no room for learner feedback is allowed. Without a system enriching function, schools and teachers are left only a modest role to play. Some don't even need formal educational institutions. In a co-figurative scenario, on the other hand, formal educational institutions are seen as central, but transmitting confused and confusing messages to the learners. The reason for this, the educators discover through the heuristic use of the table, is that both conservative forces and those pushing towards progress compete in their attempt to influence the young generation. The character of schools will vary, depending on the ideologies of their sponsors, stressing curricular content and skills, accordingly. Trainees also learn to see how in pre-figurative groups designing their culture on a day-to-day basis, creativity, self-directiveness, skill learning, ability to access, process and use large information systems become vital.

What further conclusions can TAEs reach through the use of this table? It can help them realize, for example, that both a NIS from the FSU and one from rural Ethiopia bring post-figurative attitude to their new school. This is due to the passive role allotted to learners in both communist and tribal societies. Such an insight guides the educator to take preventive action to reduce the child's trauma and make his/her transition from a post-figurative to a co-figurative school more gradual and better understand problems stemming from differential learning styles.

The use of this table as an aid to systematic holistic thinking also highlights the shift in family structure experienced by most immigrant groups to a co-figurative constellation. Youngsters who learn the new language faster are called upon to represent their parents in dealing with the authorities. The TAE also comes to understand that as in a co-figurative society so in a co-figurative family the balance of power is likely to be volatile. The extreme changes caused by immigration often induce adaptive processes closer in intensity to the pre-figurative scenario, turning all family members, young and old, into learners. Educators can play an important supportive role by helping these people see more clearly the nature and sources of the unsettling changes they are undergoing.

To help teachers better deal with various instances of NIS' antisocial behavior, they had described, such as peer violence, harming or stealing public property, I introduced and explored the applicability of such notions as "liminality" (Turner, 1970) and 'moratorium' (Erikson, 1968). NIS seem to need opportunities for boundary testing even more than "regular" adolescents in the Eriksonian developmental context, until the new norms become meaningful to them. In this light, the importance of the *Ulpan* class as a protective environment which supplies these moratorium needs, thereby facilitating gradual transition to the more rigorous climate of the *Kitot em*, becomes evident. It should be noted that prior to having gained this insight most participants saw the *Ulpan* as slowing down NIS' social integration process.

This section illustrated how a selection of anthropological concepts have been defined and operationalized in this program. Clearly, other anthropological concepts can be used in the above demonstrated format to illuminate issues relevant to the educational needs of nonimmigrant ethnic or religious minority children.

THE TEACHER-AS-ETHNOGRAPHER

The second part of the program was devoted to familiarizing participants with ethnographic research tools. Ample opportunity for practice in pertinent educational settings was provided. Intense participant input was used in designing fieldwork assignments.

Dealing with participant observation, for example, various types of observation and note-taking possibilities teachers might have in their work place were examined covering a range of situations from low to high level participation modes (Flick, 2006; Spradley, 1980: Taylor & Bogdan, 1984; Wolcott, 1999). Thus, when a TAE sets out to observe a colleague's class, he/she can adopt a passive participation style with almost unlimited note-taking possibilities. On the other hand, for a teacher observing a situation in which he/she takes an active part, such as in a professional meeting or while teaching one's own classes, the possibilities for note-taking are much more restricted. In the latter instance the teacher can rely on an observation guide drafted in advance and based on experience acquired in earlier holistic observations in the setting. In preparation for such focused participant observation, the TAE can use a variety of memory aids: from structural ones, such as graphic representation of sitting arrangements, to time sampling devices, in order to observe more dynamic aspects of classroom behavior.

One use of participant observation which trainees particularly valued was application of this research method as a mutual diagnostic tool. When a teacher encounters a classroom problem difficult to analyze because of high personal involvement, the assistance of a colleague, also trained as a TAE, can be sought. The invited TAE has to take into account the observed teacher's definition of the problem along with his/her own conclusions reached through systematic study of relevant classroom behavior and interaction patterns. The feedback the TAE provides to his/her inviting colleague can yield alternative definitions of the problem along with new suggestions for its solution. This is an additional illustration of the system enriching potential of the anthropological training model when applied on an organizational, rather than individual basis.

Much time was spent sensitizing participants to ethical considerations in ethnographic research such as informed consent, safeguarding anonymity of informants, confidentiality of privileged information, and so forth. This was done in order to make them aware of the power inherent in researchers' knowledge and also the potential for harm, if not used carefully.

The same principles of operationalization were applied in introducing and practicing various types of ethnographic interviewing, life history research, effective use of different ethnographic questions, ethnographic interview guides, basic techniques for thematic analysis of participant observation and interview data, and so forth (Agar, 1986; Gubrium & Holstein, 2002; Wolcott, 1999).

THE ETHNOGRAPHIC ACTION RESEARCH PROJECTS

Although teachers possess a large body of knowledge, it is mostly nonreplicable and nondisseminable because it is unsystematically accumulated and is not theory based (Argyris, Putnam, & Smith, 1985; Reis-Jorge, 2005; Rosiek & Atkinson, 2005; Schön, 1987). The TAE program purported to remedy this by engaging all participants in conducting research projects of their own as part of their training in the anthropological action model. These research projects allowed trainees to synthesize and apply their conceptual and methodological learning in a meaningful context. Participants were briefed to keep a log on the reflective aspects of the research process in order to study their own reactions. This increased self-awareness to research styles, revealed strengths and weaknesses, and thus contributed to the training of more effective TAEs.

Project topics chosen by participants fell into three main categories: the first concentrated on case studies, that is, explored the individual experiences of a number of NIS and their families in a variety of life situations during the first year of their cross-cultural adaptation. Phenomenological in orientation, these projects provided an insider's perspective on the process and demonstrated the direct relevance of this type of information to Teacher-Ethnographers' own in-school practice. The second category focused on issues that emerged in the course of work with immigrant youngsters whose solution necessitated a group approach. In the elementary school, teachers from the *Ulpan* and the *Kitot em* collaboratively studied the effects of NIS' daily shuttling between these two different settings. In the junior high school the principal, the psychologist, the social worker and a teacher teamed up to explore the tensions between immigrant and veteran students, caused by misunderstanding each others' expressions of adolescent sexuality and to devise ways to reduce them. In the high school, participants in the group project designed a special curriculum for the matriculation exams tailor-made for their NIS' needs. The third category dealt with administrative aspects of absorbing NIS in the school system.

All projects included three different levels of discourse. The first was the descriptive one, on which the documentation of observed phenomena occurred. The second was the interpretive level, on which participants attempted to explain the phenomena, applying the various theoretical frameworks studied. On the third level, using an inductive approach, they explored conditions under which cautious cross-setting generalization of findings would be feasible.

Though limitations of space preclude a substantive treatment of project outcomes, to conclude this section it can be stated that through these projects trainees learned the building blocks of scientific practice: to critically assess the reliability of information sources, to experience the heuristic use of theory, and to systematically present data and report findings.

WHERE DOES THIS TAKE US

Learning occurs at various levels of comprehension and commitment. Spiro (1966), in his acclaimed article "Buddhism and Economic Action in Burma" (p. 1164), developed a five-stage scale to explain the acquisition of new cultural concepts. It comprises: "learning about, understanding, believing, using the belief to organize or account for behavior, and internalizing the concept as an important element in the actor's motivational system." Stages one and two refer to the learner's cognitive attitude to the new content presented. At stages three and four comprehension is followed by acceptance, that is, affective level change occurs. Finally, it is adopted and becomes an integral part of the learner's behavioral repertoire. No longer having to think about it, he/she will now act intuitively.

This anthropological action-research model provided a learning experience at all five levels. Participants were exposed to new knowledge. The evaluation of the intervention indicates that they came to accept it as both reliable and convincing. Having also obtained operative tools, they started to reorganize their daily work accordingly. Through the implementation of the action research project they had the opportunity to experiment with this new knowledge and adopt it. Internalization relates to long-term effects of change, hence the question whether the different trainees reached this stage can only be answered with confidence after a further period of time. However, the two-phase program evaluation that took place at the end of the intervention and 1 year later (combining individual and group interviews and observations at the work place), indicated that most of the participants tended toward the optimal end of the continuum. Moreover, several expressed interest in pursuing graduate studies in educational anthropology.

A basic assumption of this model is that since culturally different students' needs constantly change, educators should be able to devise ways to meet them. The TAE model implies, then, a liberal conception of curriculum, largely locally determined. It also implies professional accountability, accomplished through ongoing self-evaluation. In spelling out their postmodernist creed on program evaluation, Guba and Lincoln (1989) maintain that the truth of the evaluator is no more than just another perspective, as there is no one objective reality. Accordingly, our program emphasizes the provision of skills for self-assessment of goals and performance as a means to achieving and perpetuating reflective practice (Harrison, Lawson, & Wortley, 2005; Pedro, 2006).

The essence of what is considered good in-service training is determined by the underlying conception of the desirable educational change (Konings, Brand-Gruwel, & van Merrienboer, 2007; Mathison, 1992). House (1981), in his influential treatise, makes a more elaborate distinction by differentiating between three perspectives on educational change or innovation: the technological, the political, and the cultural. The first emphasizes the introduction of new techniques and takes an instrumental stance toward teachers, whose only allotted role is to channel the change to their students. It should be noted that most centralized educational reforms share this outcome versus process orientation (Sleeter, 1992; Swanson, 2005). The second interprets educational innovation politically and gives special consideration to the position of various community interest groups. The cultural approach takes a more contextualized view of institutional change as the product of negotiation between the different subcultures that make up any complex social organization.

Research highlights that educators need the most support when they try to implement new methods or innovations, regardless of the amount of time they have spent in in-service training prior to that (Fullan, 1991; McGrail, 2006). The TAE model creates for the trainees an integrated learning continuum between the program and the school. Adopting a cultural approach to educational innovation, following House's (1981) typology, the effectiveness of the present intervention program fosters a holistic perception of institutional change.

McDiarmid (1992), in analyzing and critically assessing the "Multicultural Week Program" conducted by the Los Angeles Unified School District, alerts us to the inadequacy of information provision as a means of attitude change. Instead of uprooting generalizations and stereotypes about ethnic groups, such programs result in strengthening them, he claims. The TAE model, on the other hand, offers concepts and methods as well as opportunities to collect, interpret and apply information.

Cazden and Meehan (1989), McDiarmid (1992) and Nordhoff and Kleinfeld (1993) underscore the importance of furnishing prospective teachers with experiential learning opportunities about their future students' lives and histories. The training program outlined here facilitates meaningful future application through the organization of skills and conceptual tools into a cohesive anthropological model. The analogy between the teacher and the ethnographer inherently functions as a catalyst for such future utilization. The anthropologist presents a vivid role model for both practicing and prospective teachers to follow.

Although the TAE model has been conceptualized for in-service level training, it is adaptable to preservice training, as well. Practice teaching can be perceived as a "double field work" experience. Based on modeling, apprentice teaching is an efficient means for role socialization. The TAE model supplies a complementary route to professional socialization, with the ethnographer serving as an alternative role model. Interpreting "field work" not in a practicum, but in an anthropological sense, the teacher trainee is invited to explore the new school as an anthropologist learns to understand a foreign culture. This approach affords a holistic perspective on the school: its organizational structure, the symbols, languages, as well as overall communicative codes of its various subsystems, and launches the prospective teacher on a career of reflective practice, following the principles presented in this model.

The application of this model will, in all likelihood, enhance the positive role teachers can play in promoting synergistic coexistence between immigrant and local students. The TAE model promises to be a salutary tool empowering schools and their staffs to foster unimpeded exchange of ideas among young people from various cultural backgrounds so as to better serve the ever changing and emerging needs of an increasingly globalized world. Indeed, Teachers-as-Ethnographers carry both the mindset and the skills to turn cultural diversity into a cornucopia for generations to come.

NOTES

1. The intervention described in this paper was funded by the Israeli Ministry of Education. The graduate research assistants who participated in the

team were: Mira Karnieli, Yossi Mamman, Michelle Trope, later replaced by Anat Kedem.

2. Although on one level the term "Teacher-as-Ethnographer" (TAE) differentiates between the conceptual and methodological aspects of training, TAE is generically used in this chapter to refer to participants in the program, graduates, or even prospective future users. It includes all other educational functions such as administrators, educational counselors, school psychologists, social workers, and so forth. TAE, as an acronym, always refers to the action model itself.

A PROGRAMMATIC EPILOGUE

This volume has been devoted to the description and analysis of the experiences of first generation (also referred to as "one-and-a-half generations") Russian youth in Israel, as an illustration of a group of immigrants who excel. I highlighted their encounters in various environments in the new country, their adjustment in formal and informal settings, while stressing gender differences and looking for different profiles within the broader category of adaptation styles; this was in order to bring out intragroup variance. Although my insights are based on in-depth phenomenological studies, and ample room has to be allowed for the expression and celebration of individual differences, the likelihood of these findings to be cautiously generalizable to this population at large is high. The prescriptive mode of socialization to which they had been exposed accounts for the group members' intense norm compliance.

I tried to underscore their strengths and weaknesses analyzing underlying motives for both. While concentrating on Russian immigrant youths in Israel, I tried to present their various features comparatively with other high achievers, particularly Transylvanians in Israel, Punjabis, and Central Americans in the United States, in order to gain an understanding of unique, along with common attributes of such immigrant youth.

As I have earlier demonstrated, immigrant youth have a higher propensity to become globalists than their local peers. Let us now proceed to illuminate how the encounter between immigrants and locals can be used to enhance global participation skills of both constituents. Reiterated

Immigrant Youth Who Excel: Globalization's Uncelebrated Heroes, pp. 151–154
Copyright © 2008 by Information Age Publishing

in the introduction was the point that these talented youths had theoretically better chances to make a dent on their host society than most immigrants elsewhere, because of their size relative to the host society, confidence in their cultural endowment and favorable attitude of the receivers. Nevertheless, as I have indicated in the various chapters, in spite of the aforementioned positive "opening conditions," these high achievers also had shortcomings that impeded their potential to become precursors of globalization.

There are preconditions for globalization fitness to be enhanced through intercultural encounters between immigrants and locals in receiving societies. To examine how the three participating entities: immigrants who excel, local students, and teachers should optimally collaborate to make these encounters fruitful, we should start by considering problem areas each exhibits. Deterred by a sense of deficit in power balance vis-à-vis local peers, immigrants are hesitant to initiate intergroup rapprochement. Locals do not perceive lack of contact as a loss, whereas the problem teachers face, as pointed out in chapter 5, is replacing the assimilationist model by a Teacher-as-Ethnographer approach (chapter 7). Without such a shift in teacher attitudes, no collaboration is feasible. It is their role, as representatives of formal education systems, to bring the parties together. This is the case since the functions for which they need to train the young are also to be played out in formal, as opposed to private or informal contexts, that is, at the work place. Teachers should identify immigrant youths' aptitudes and convey to local students, through personal example, appreciation for them.

They should seek to acquaint both groups with the globalist scene, the principles and working style characteristic of a globalized economy for which they have to prepare. They should stress that this is for all, including teachers themselves, an exercise in prefigurative cultural planning, to use Margaret Mead's term—a new model for coexistence in which all learn, as explained in chapter 7. Visits to globalized firms and corporations, assisted by virtual visits to more remote globalized sites could effectively expose youths to this reality and stimulate their creativity. The intercultural work ethos of these corporations could make them realize the advantages of immigrant-local interaction in school, as a lead-in to such a lifestyle. Under the inspiration of these visits, youth could be encouraged to design joint research/work projects, choose their topics, role play them, as well as construct scenarios for their real life application. These activities readily provide opportunities for the creation of task forces—based on the talents of various participants—through which they can learn to value each others' skills and capitalize on them: rotate leadership at various stages of the projects; construct mixed-gender teams in order to benefit from female members' identified assets, such as superior social and language abilities.

Teachers-as-Ethnographers (TAEs) should accompany, advise, facilitate, provide feedback, suggest sources, here and there, but on the whole, limit their input to low level participation. For example, TAEs could assist in team formation to render their composition complementary without stereotyping any of the members, immigrants or locals. They could conduct work logs that will enable evaluation of the projects, participation styles of individual members and their contributions. Presentation of projects across teams and to additional in-school audiences will enhance within-team unity, exchange of information and improve members' rhetorical skills. Teams with outstanding projects should be urged to submit them, with detailed budgets, to venture capitalists in order to gain insight into the intricacies of global marketing. TAEs should direct teams how to put projects together from various components. Direct them how to put a team project together from various components, seek and receive help from consultants, as needed, investigating where such help is located. They should make it clear that these are not forced exercises in integration and emphasize that beyond the joint projects, participants should be able to continue their life routine. Thus, members can maintain their group and personal boundaries, giving expression to their ethnic or situational identities. Segmentation, cooperation and flow—experienced and performed simultaneously—define globalized life style, both when it comes to work and participants' identity construction.

Teachers of various disciplines should also work together to follow the trajectories of various students and help them along their course of learning globalized lifestyles. Team work and intercultural group projects offer students an exceptional opportunity to grasp the importance of mutuality, respect for different styles and talents of their peers in an in vivo context.

All should be advised to use their cultural endowment for the enrichment of the projects. Shared interest in the latter's success makes an eclectic approach to knowledge prevail. The message conveyed is that the source of information, knowledge or skill does not constitute grounds for its ranking, as long as it advances the common goal. These involvements are likely to expand, turning intercultural teams into organic learning communities.

If participants of one group choose to spend time with members of the other group beyond the projects, TAEs should be supportive but refrain from any kind of interference. While students should be asked to record, evaluate and, in general, strive for higher level of reflectivity on task-related activities, voluntary get-togethers should be left completely unsupervised by adults.

This operational model of intercultural collaboration is applicable with due adjustments in immigrant receiving communities, provided that educators are willing to adopt a TAE approach to assist their local and immigrant students to work together in the manner detailed above. The model provides a natural context for the two groups' members to get to know each other around a task, a challenge that is new to both of them, thereby offering an egalitarian starting point. This is crucial in light of the fact that ignorance and stereotypes about the other group's lifestyle dominate the scene on both sides, leading youths to hold defensive positions accompanied by exclusionary tendencies. Since this model gives the two parties an opportunity to bring out their capacities, thereby gaining mutual appreciation, each will be more likely to recognize their own drawbacks, and admit the other group members' fortes. For example, locals will acknowledge immigrants' more focused future orientation, higher ability to handle change, reflectiveness, and multilingualism. At the same time, immigrants will be confronted with their often unduly judgmental attitude towards persons and institutions in the host society fueled by misunderstandings they base on imported preconceptions. Genuine self-appraisal is a precondition for deepening of intergroup cooperation. It takes the initiative of TAEs to orchestrate all this and make participation in such an exciting, globalization-oriented school experience rewarding for all actors: locals, immigrants, and not least, educators themselves

REFERENCES

Abedi, J. (2004). The No Child Left Behind Act and English language learners: Assessment and accountability issue. *Educational Researcher, 33*(1), 1–14.

Addi-Raccah, A. (2005). Gender and teachers' attrition: The occupational destination of former teachers. *Sex Roles, 53,* 739–750.

Agar, M. (1986). *Speaking of ethnography.* Beverly Hills: SAGE.

Al-Haj, M. (2002). Identity patterns among immigrants from the former Soviet Union in Israel: Assimilation vs. ethnic formation. *International Migration, 40*(2), 49–70.

Allan, R., & Hill, B. (1995). Multicultural education in Australia: Historical development and current status. In J. A. Banks & C. A. M. Banks (Eds.), *Handbook of research on multicultural education* (pp. 763–777). New York: Macmillan.

Anderson, E. (1994). A new look at an old construct: Cross-cultural adaptation. *International Journal of Intercultural Relations, 18*(3), 293-327.

Argyris, C., Putnam, R., & Smith, D. M. (1985). *Action science.* San Francisco: Jossey-Bass.

Aronowitz, M. (1984). The social and emotional adjustment of immigrant children: A review of the literature. *International Migration Review, 18*(2), 237–257.

Aronowitz, M. (1992). Adjustment of immigrant children as a function of parental attitudes to change. *International Migration Review, 26*(1), 89–110.

Attwood, L. (1990). *The new Soviet man and woman: Studies in Soviet history and society.* London: Macmillan.

Azarya, V., & Kimmerling, B. (1983). New immigrants in the Israeli armed forces. *Armed Forces and Society, 6,* 455–482.

Azaryahu, M. (1999). The Independence Day military parade: A political history of a patriotic ritual. In E. Lomsky-Feder & E. Ben-Ari (Eds.), *The military and militarism in Israeli society* (pp. 89–116). Albany: The State University of New York Press.

Babbie, E. (2004). *The practice of social research* (10th ed.) Belmont, CA: Thomson-Wadsworth.

Banks, J. A. (2001). Multicultural education: Characteristics and goals. In J. A. Banks & C. A. M. Banks (Eds.), *Multicultural education: Issues and perspectives* (4th ed., pp. 1–30). New York: Wiley.

Bardach, R. (2005). Israel: A country of immigration. In *World migration 2005: Cost and benefits of international migration*. Geneva: International Organization for Migration.

Basok, T. (2002). Fragmented identities: The case of former Soviet Jews in Toronto. *Identity: An International Journal of Theory and Research, 2*(4), 341–360.

Bauman, Z. (1998). *Globalization: The human consequences*. London: Polity Press.

Ben-Ari, E. (1998). *Mastering soldiers: Conflict, emotions and the enemy in an Israeli military unit*. Oxford, England: Berghahn.

Ben-Rafael, E. (1982). *The emergency of ethnicity*. Westport, CT: Greenwood Press.

Ben-Shalom, U., & Horenczyk, G. (2004). Cultural identity and adaptation in an assimilative setting: Immigrant soldiers from the former Soviet Union in Israel. *International Journal of Intercultural Relations, 28*(6), 461–479.

Ben-Yehuda, N. (1999. The Masada mythical narrative and the Israeli army. In E. Lomsky-Feder & E. Ben-Ari (Eds.), *The military and militarism in Israeli society*. New York: SUNY.

Bertaux, D. (Ed.). (1981). *Biography and society: The life history approach in the social sciences*. Beverly Hills, CA: Sage.

Bhatia, S., & Ram, A. (2001). Rethinking "acculturation" in relation to diasporic cultures and postcolonial identities. *Human Development, 44*(1), 1–18.

Blair, H. (2004). Jump-starting democracy: Adult civic education and democratic participation in three countries. *Democratization, 10*(1), 53–76.

Bloch, M. N., Kennedy, D., Lightfoot, T., & Weynberg, D. (Eds.). (2006). *The child in the world/The world in the child*. New York: Palgrave.

Borg, M. G., Riding, R. J., & Falzon, J. M. (1991). Stress in teaching: A study of occupational stress and its determinants, job satisfaction and career commitment among primary school teachers. *Educational Psychology, 11*, 59–75.

Borgatti, S. P. (1993). Cultural domain analysis. *Journal of Quantitative Anthropology, 4*(4), 261–278.

Bourdieu, P. (1986). L'Illusion biographique [The biographic illusion]. *Acts de la Recherche en Sciences Sociales, 62*(3), 69–72.

Bourdieu, P. (1990). La domination masculine [Male domination]. *Actes de la Recherche en Sciences Sociales, 84*, 3–31.

Brah, A. (1992). Difference, diversity and differentiation. In J. Donald & A. Rattansi (Eds.), *Race, culture and difference*. London: SAGE.

Brettell, C. (2000). Theorizing migration in anthropology. In C. B. Brettell & J. F. Hollifield (Eds.), *Migration theory: Talking across disciplines* (pp. 97–136). New York: Routledge.

Bronfenbrenner, U. (1970). *Two worlds of childhood*. New York: Basic Books.

Brown, B. B., Larson, R., & Sarawathi, T. S. (Eds.). (2002). *Introduction. The world's youth: Adolescence in eight regions of the globe* (pp. 1–15). New York: Cambridge University Press.

Burke, R. J., & Greenglass, E. (1993). The clients' role in psychological burnout in teachers and administrators. *Psychological Report, 64*, 1299–1306.

Burton, L. (1990). *Gender and mathematics: An international perspective*. Strand: Cassell.

Butler, R. J., & Gasson, S. L. (2005). Self esteem and self concept scales for children and adolescents. *Children and Adolescent Mental Health, 10*(4), 190–201.

Byrne, B. M. (1994). Burnout: Testing for the validity and invariance of causal structure across elementary, intermediate and secondary teachers. *American Educational Research Journal, 31*, 645–673.

Cahan, S., Davis, D., & Staub, R. (2001). Age at immigration and scholastic achievement in school-age children: Is there a vulnerable age? *International Migration Review, 35*(2), 587–593.

Cameron, D. (1998). Gender, language and discourse: A review essay. *Signs, 1*, 945–973.

Carmeli, A., & Fadlon, J. (1997). Motivation to serve in the Israeli army: the gap between cultural involvement and cultural performance. In N. Lewin-Epstein, Y. Roi, & P. Ritterband (Eds.), *Russian Jews on three continents: Migration and resettlement* (pp. 389–405). London: Frank Cass.

Cazden, C., & Mehan, H. (1989). Principles from sociology and anthropology: Context, code, classroom and culture. In M. Reynolds (Ed.), *Knowledge base for the beginning teacher*. Oxford, England: Pergamon Press.

Chaffe, S. H., Nass, C. S., & Yang, S. M. (1990). The bridging role of television in immigrant political soicialization. *Human Communication Research, 17*(2), 266-288.

Clark, C., & Uzzell, D. L. (2002). The affordances of the home, neighborhood, school and town center for adolescents. *Journal of Environmental Psychology, 22*, 95–108.

Clark, C., & Uzzell, D. L. (2006). The socio-environmental affordances of adolescents' environments. In C. Spencer & M. Blades (Eds.), *Children and their environments: Learning, using, designing spaces* (pp. 176–195). Cambridge, England: Cambridge University Press.

Claussen, B., & Mueller, H. (2000). *Political socialization of the young in East and West*. Frankfurt, Germany: Verlag Peter Lang.

Cohen, C. (1994). Facing job loss: Changing relationships in a multicultural urban factory. In L. Lamphere, A. Stepick, & G. Grenier (Eds.), *Newcomers in the workplace: Immigrants and the restructuring of the U.S. economy* (pp. 231–250). Philadelphia: Temple University Press.

Cohen, S. A. (1995). The Israel Defense Forces (IDF): From a "People's Army" to a "Professional Military"—Causes and implications. *Armed Forces and Society, 21*(2, Winter), 237–254.

Cohen, S. A. (1997). Towards a new portrait of a (new) Israeli soldier. *Israel Affairs, 3*(Spring/Summer), 77–117.

Crul, M. (2007). The integration of immigrant youth. In M. Suárez-Orozco (Ed.), *Learning in a global era: International perspectives on globalization and education* (pp. 213–231). Berkeley: University of California Press.

Dane, F. R. (1990). *Research methods*. Pacific Grove: Brooks/Cole.

Deegan, J. (1993). Gender and pedagogy in Soviet education: The inherited context. *International Education Journal, 22*(2), 46–57.

Della Pergola, S. (2004). Demographic trends in Israel and Palestine: Prospects and policy implications. In D. Singer & L. Grossman (Eds.), *American Jewish year book* (pp. 3–70). New York: American Jewish Committee.

Denzin, N., & Lincoln, Y. (1994). Introduction: Entering the field of qualitative research. In *Handbook of qualitative research* (pp. 1–17). Newbury Park, CA: SAGE.

Dolan, K. (1995). Attitudes, behaviors and the influence of the family: A reexamination of the role of family structure. *Political Behavior, 17*(3), 251–264.

Dressler, W. W., Borges, C. D., Balieiro, M. C., & dos Santos, J. E. (2005). Measuring cultural consonance: Examples with special reference to measurement theory in anthropology. *Field Methods, 17*(4), 331–355.

Dudley, R., & Gitelson, A. R. (2002). Political literacy, civic education, and civic engagement: A return to political socialization? *Applied Developmental Science, 6*(4), 175–182.

Eisikovits, R. A. (1995a). An anthropological action model for training teachers to work with culturally different student populations. *Educational Action Research, 3*(3), 263–277.

Eisikovits, R. A. (1995b). "I'll tell you what school should do for us": How immigrant youths from the former USSR. view their high school experience in Israel. *Youth and Society, 27*(2), 230–255.

Eisikovits, R. A. (1995c). Educational success and long-term adaptation of immigrant students: An Israeli perspective. *International Journal of Qualitative Studies in Education, 8*(2), 171–181.

Eisikovits, R. A. (1997). The educational experience and performance of immigrant and minority students in Israel. *Anthropology and Education Quarterly, 28*, 394–410.

Eisikovits, R. A. (2000). Gender differences in cross-cultural adaptation styles of immigrant youths from the former USSR in Israel. *Youth and Society, 31*(3), 310–331.

Eisikovits, R. A. (2005). Perspectives of young immigrants from the former USSR. on voting and politics in Israel. *Theory and Research in Social Education, 33*(4), 454–475.

Eisikovits, R. A. (2006). Intercultural learning among Russian immigrant recruits in the Israeli army. *Armed Forces and Society, 32*(2), 292–306.

Eisikovits, R. A. (2008). Coping with high achieving transnational immigrant students: The experience of Israeli teachers. *Teaching and Teacher Education, 24*(2), 277–289.

Eisikovits, R. A., & Beck, R. H. (1990). Models governing the education of new immigrant students in Israel. *Comparative Education Review, 34*(2), 177–195.

Eisikovits, R. A., Hedin, D. P., & Adam, V. (1984). Political participation: A comparative view of Israeli and American youths. *Children and Youth Services Review, 6*(1), 47–64.

Eisikovits, R. A., & Karnieli, M. (1992). Acquiring conflict resolution skills as cultural learning: An Israeli example. *Higher Education, 23*(2), 183–194.

Eldering, L. (1996). Multiculturalism and multicultural education in an international perspective. *Anthropology and Education Quarterly, 27*(3), 315–330.

Eldering, L. (1997). Ethnic minority students in the Netherlands from a cultural-ecological perspective. *Anthropology and Education Quarterly, 28*(3), 330–350.

Eldering, L., & Kloprogge, J. (Eds.). (1989). *Different cultures, same schools: Ethnic minority children in Europe*. Amsterdam: Swets & Zeitlinger.

Eldering, L., & Knorth, E. J. (1998). Immigrant adolescents in residential group care and treatment settings: Research and experience in the Netherlands. *Child & Youth Care Forum, 27*(4), 237–259.

Entwisle, D. (1990). Schools and the adolescent. In S. Feldman & G. Elliott (Eds.), *At the threshold: The developing adolescent*. Cambridge, MA: Harvard University Press.

Erikson, E. (1968). *Identity: Youth and crisis*. New York: Norton.

Ernst, G., & Statzner. E. (1994). Alternative visions of schooling: An introduction. *Anthropology & Education Quarterly. 25*(3), 200–207.

Feldman S., & Elliott, G. (Eds.). (1990). *At the threshold: The developing adolescent*. Cambridge, MA: Harvard University Press.

Figueroa, P. (1995). Multicultural education in the United Kingdom: Historical development and current states. In J. A. Banks & C. A. M. Banks (Eds.), *Handbook of research on multicultural education* (pp. 778–800). New York: Macmillan.

Fine, M., Burns, A., Payne, Y., & Torre, M. (2004). Civic lessons: The color and class of betrayal. *Teacher College Record, 106*, 2193–2223.

Fine, M., Reva, J., Pedraza, P., Futch, V., & Stoudt, B. (2007). Swimming: On oxygen, resistance, and possibility for immigrant youth under siege. *Anthropology & Education Quarterly, 38*(12), 76–96.

Fitzgerald, J. K. (1974). Introduction. In *Social and cultural identity* (pp. 1–4). Atlanta, GA: Southern Anthropological Society, University of Georgia Press.

Flanagan, C. (2003). Developmental roots of political engagement. *Political Science and Politics, 36*(2), 257–261.

Flick, U. (2006). *An introduction to qualitative research* (3rd ed.). London: SAGE.

Fontana, A., & Frey, J. (1994). Interviewing: The art of science. In N. Denzin & Y. Lincoln (Eds.), *Handbook of qualitative research*. Newbury Park. CA: SAGE.

Frankrijker, H. (1997). The challenge of teacher education in and for a plural world. *Teaching and Teacher Education, 13*(6), 659–664.

Freeman, D., Brookhart, S. M., & Loadman, W. E. (1999). Realities of teaching in racially/ethnically diverse schools: Feedback from entry-level teachers. *Urban Education, 34*(1), 89–114.

Fullan, M. G. (1991). *The new meaning of educational change* (2nd ed.) New York: Teachers College Press.

Galston, W. (2001). Political knowledge, political engagement, and civic education. *Annual Review of Political Science, 4*, 217–234.

Galston, W. (2004). Civic education and political participation. *Political Science and Politics, 37*(2), 263–266.

Gibson. M. (1988). *Accommodation without assimilation: Sikh immigrants in an American high school.* Ithaca, NY: Cornell University Press.

Gibson, M. (1991). Minorities and schooling: Some implications. In M. Gibson & J. Ogbu (Eds.), *Minority status and schooling: A comparative study of immigrant and involuntary minorities.* New York: Garland.

Gibson, M. (1995). Additive acculturation as a strategy for school improvement. In R. Rumbaut & W. Cornelius (Eds.), *California's immigrant children: Theory, research, and implications for educational policy* (pp. 58–70). San Diego, CA: La Jolla, Center for U.S.-Mexican Studies, University of California.

Gibson, M. (1997). Complicating the immigrant/involuntary typology. *Anthropology and Education Quarterly, 28*(3), 431–454.

Gibson, M. A. (2001). Immigrant adaptation and patterns of acculturation. *Human Development, 44*(1), 19–23.

Gibson M. A., & Ogbu. J. U. (Eds.). (1991). *Minority status and schooling: A comparative study of immigrant and involuntary minorities.* New York: Garland.

Gifford, C. (2004). National and post-national dimensions of citizenship education in the U.K. *Citizenship Studies, 8*(2), 145–158.

Gillborn, D. (1997). Ethnicity and educational performance in the United Kingdom: Racism, ethnicity, and variability in achievement. *Anthropology & Education Quarterly, 28*(3), 375–393.

Gillborn, D., & Gipps, C. (1996). *Review of recent research on the achievements of ethnic minority pupils.* London: Office for Standards in Education.

Giordano, P. (2003). Relationships in adolescence. *Annual Review of Sociology, 29*, 257–281.

Glick-Schiller, N., Basch, L., & Blanc-Szanton, C. (1995). From immigrant to transmigrant: Theorizing transnational migration. *Anthropological Quarterly, 68*, 48–63.

Glynn, C., Hayes, A., & Shanahan, J. (1997). Perceived support for one's opinions and willingness to speak out: A meta-analysis of survey studies on the spiral of silence. *Public Opinion Quarterly, 61*, 452–463.

Guba, E. G., & Lincoln, Y. S. (1989). *Fourth generation evaluation.* Newbury Park, CA: SAGE.

Gubrium, J. F., & Holstein, J. A. (Eds.) (2002). *Handbook of interview research.* Thousand Oaks, CA: SAGE.

Hall, C. (1992). *White, male and middle class: Explorations in feminism and history.* London: Polity Press.

Harrison, J., Lawson, T., & Wortley, A. (2005). Facilitating the professional learning of new teachers through critical reflection on practice during mentoring meetings. *European Journal of Teacher Education, 28*(3), 267–292.

Haste, H. (2004). Constructing the citizen. *Political Psychology, 25*(3), 413–439.

Helman, S. (1999). Militarism and the construction of the life-world of Israeli males: The case of the reserves system: In E. Lomsky-Feder & E. Ben-Ari

(Eds.), *The military and militarism in Israeli Society* (pp. 191–221). New York: SUNY.

Hess, D. (2002). Discussing controversial public issues in secondary social studies classrooms. *Theory and Research in Social Education, 30*, 10–41.

Hollis, S. (2004). Blaming me, blaming you: Assessing service learning and participants' tendency to blame the victim. *Sociological Spectrum, 24*(5), 575–600.

Holstein, J. A., & Gubrium, J. F. (1994). Phenomenology, ethnomethodology, and interpretive practice. In N. Denzin & Y. Lincoln (Eds.), *Handbook of qualitative research* (pp. 262–272). Newbury Park, CA: SAGE.

Horowitz, T. (Ed.). (1989). *The Soviet man in an open society.* New York: University Press of America.

Horowitz, T. (1994). The influence of Soviet political culture on immigrant voters in Israel: The elections of 1992. *Jews in Eastern Europe, 1*(23), 5–22.

House, E. R. (1981). Three perspectives on innovation: technological, political and cultural. In R. Lehming & M. Kane (Eds.), *Improving schools* (pp. 17–41). Beverly Hills, CA: SAGE.

Hurh, W., & Kim, K. (1984). Adhesive sociocultural adaptation of Korean immigrants in the U.S.: An alternative strategy of minority adaptation. *International Migration Review, 18*(2), 188–216.

Ichilov, O. (1991). Political socialization and schooling effects among Israeli adolescents. *Comparative Education Review, 35*(3), 430–446.

Ichilov, O. (Ed.). (1998). *Citizenship and citizenship education in a changing world.* London: Woburn Press.

Ichilov, O. (2003). Teaching civics in a divided society: The case of Israel. *International Studies in the Sociology of Education, 13*(3), 219–241.

Ichilov, O., Bar-Tal, D., & Mazawi, A. (1989). Israeli adolescents' comprehension of and evaluation of democracy. *Youth and Society, 21*(2), 153–169.

Ima, K. (1995). Testing the American dream: Case studies of at-risk southeast Asian refugee students in secondary schools. In R. Rumbaut & W. Cornelius (Eds.), *California's immigrant children: Theory, research, and implications for educational policy* (pp. 191–208). San Diego, CA: La Jolla, Center for U.S.-Mexican Studies, University of California.

Johansson, O. (1991). Youth and mass media: On the co-variation between mass media use and democratic values. *Politics and the Individual, 1*(1), 49–65.

Kahane, R. (1986). Informal agencies of socialization and the integration of immigrant youth, into society: An example from Israel. *International Migration Review, 20*(1), 210–239.

Kahane, R., & Rapoport, T. (1990). Informal youth movements and the generation of democratic experience: An Israeli experience. In O. Ichilov (Ed.), *Political socialization, citizenship education and democracy* (pp. 221–240). New York: Teachers College Press.

Kao, G., & Tienda, M. (1995). Optimism and achievement: The educational performance of immigrant youth. *Social Science Quarterly 76*(1), 1–19.

Kaplan, D., & Manners, A. (1972). *Culture theory.* Englewood Cliffs, NJ: Prentice Hall.

Kearney, M. (1995). The local and the global: The anthropology of globalization and transnationalism. *Annual Review of Anthropology, 24*, 547–565.

Kibria, N. (2003). *Becoming Asian American: Second-generation Chinese and Korean American identities*. Baltimore: Johns Hopkins University Press.

Kilman, C. (2005). Crossing borders/border crossings. *Teaching tolerance, 28*, 26–30.

King, E. (1973). *Other schools and ours*. London: Holt, Reinhart and Winston.

Konings, K. D., Brand-Gruwel, S., & van Merrienboer, J. J. G. (2007). Teachers' perspectives on innovations: Implications for educational design. *Teaching and Teacher Education, 23*(6), 985–997.

Korpella, K. (2002). Children's environments. In R. B. Bechtel & A. Churchman (Eds.), *Handbook of environmental psychology* (pp. 363–373). New York: Wiley.

Kottak, C. P. (2002). *Cultural anthropology*. Boston: McGraw-Hill.

Kovács, M. L., & Cropley, A. J. (1975). *Immigrants and society*. Sydney, Australia: McGraw-Hill.

Lanir, Z. (1991). Educating for democratic behaviour in an intercultural context. *International Journal of Intercultural Relations, 15*, 327-343.

LeCompte, M., & Preisslc, J. (with Tesch, R.). (1993). *Ethnography and qualitative design in educational research* (2nd ed.). New York: Academic Press.

Lee, S. J. (1996). *Unraveling the "model minority" stereotype: Listening to Asian American youth*. New York: Teachers College Press.

Leiding, D. (2007). Planning multicultural lessons. *Principal Leadership, 8*(1), 48–51.

Lewellen, T. C. (2002). *The anthropology of globalization*. Westport, CT: Bergin & Garvey.

Liebes, T., & Ribak, R. (1992). The contribution of family culture to political participation, political outlook, and its reproduction. *Communication Research, 19*(5), 618–641.

Lieblich, A. (1993). Looking at change: Natasha, 21: New immigrant from Russia to Israel. In R. Josselson & A. Lieblich (Eds.), *The narrative study of lives* (pp. 92–129). Newbury Park, CA: SAGE.

Lieblich, A., & Perlow, M. (1988). Transition to adulthood during military service. *The Jerusalem Quarterly, 47*(Summer), 40–78.

Macdonald, D. (1999). Teacher attrition: A review of literature. *Teaching and Teacher Education, 15*, 835–848.

Markowitz, F. (1996). "Shopping" for the future: Cultural change, border crossing, and identity options of Jewish teenagers from the C.I.S. *Ethos, 24*(2), 350–373.

Markowitz, F. (2000). *Coming of age in post-Soviet Russia*. Urbana, IL: University of Illinois Press.

Marris. P. (1980). The uprooting of meaning. In G. Coelho & P. Ahmed (Eds.), *Uprooting and development: Dilemmas of coping and modernization* (pp. 101–116). New York: Plenum.

Mathison, S. (1992). An evaluation model for inservice teacher education. *Evaluation and Program Planning, 15*, 255–261.

Maynard, M. (1994). "Race," gender and the concept of "difference" in feminist thought. In H. Afshar & M. Maynard (Eds.), *The dynamics of "race" and "gender": Some feminist intervention* (pp. 9–25). London: Taylor & Francis.

McAndrew, M. (2007). The education of immigrant students in a globalized world: Policy debates in a comparative perspective. In M. Suárez-Orozco (Ed.), *Learning in a global era: International perspectives on globalization and education* (pp. 232–255). Berkeley: University of California Press.

McCormick, J. (1997). Occupational stress of teachers: Biographical differences in a large school system. *Journal of Educational Administration*, *35*, 18–38.

McDiarmid. G. W. (1992). What to do about differences? A study of multicultural education for teacher trainees in the Los Angeles Unified School District. *Journal of Teacher Education*, *43*, 83–93.

McGrail, E. (2006). "It's a double-edged sword, this technology business": Secondary English teachers' perspectives on a schoolwide laptop technology initiative. *Teachers College Record, 108*(6), 1055–1079.

McLeod, J. (2000). Media and civic socialization of youth. *Journal of Adolescent Health, 27*, 45–51.

McNeil, L. (2005). Faking equity: High stakes testing and the education of Latino youth. In A. Valenzuela (Ed.), *Leaving children behind: How "Texas-style" accountability fails Latino youth* (pp. 57–112). Albany: University of New York Press.

Mead, M. (1970). *Culture and commitment: The study of the generation gap*. New York: Garden City.

Mead, M. (n.d.). *Four Families* [Film]. Delmar, CA: CRM McGraw-Hill Films.

Milner, H. (2002). *Civic literacy: How informed citizens make democracy work*. Hanover, NH: University Press of New England.

Mirsky, L., & Kaushinsky, F. (1989). Migration and growth: Separation-individuation process in immigrant students in Israel. *Adolescence. 24*, 725–740.

Moustakas, C. (1994), *Phenomenological research methods*. Thousand Oaks, CA: SAGE.

Muckle, J. (1990). *Portrait of a Soviet school under Glasnost,* New York: St. Martin's.

Ngo, B. (2006). Learning from the margins: The education of Southeast and South Asian Americans in context. *Race, Ethnicity and Education, 9*(1), 51–65.

Niemi, R. G., Hepburn, M. A., & Chapman, C. (2000). Community service by high school students: A cure for civic ills? *Political Behavior, 22*(1), 45–69.

Nieto, S. (1995). A history of the education of Puerto Rican students in the U.S. mainland schools: "Losers," "outsiders," or "leaders"? In J. A. Banks & C. A. M. Banks (Eds.), *Handbook of Research on Multicultural Education* (pp. 388–411). New York: Macmillan.

Nieto, S. (Ed.). (1999). *The light in their eyes: Creating multicultural learning communities*. New York: Teachers College Press.

Nordhoff, K., & Kleinfeld. J. (1993). Preparing teachers for multicultural classrooms. *Teaching and Teacher Education, 9*, 27–39.

O'Dunivin, K. (1994). Military culture: Change and continuity. *Armed Forces and Society, 20*(4), 531–547.

Ogbu, J. U., & Simons, H. D. (1998). Voluntary and involuntary minorities: A cultural-ecological theory of school performance with some implications for education. *Anthropology & Education Quarterly, 29*(2), 155–188.

Otoya-Knapp, K. (2005). More than I bargained for: Confronting biases in teacher preparation. *Teacher Education and Practice, 18*(1), 15–34.

Pang, V. O. (2006). Fighting the marginalization of Asian American students with caring schools: Focusing on curriculum change. *Race, Ethnicity and Education, 3*(1), 67–83.

Pearson, L. (1990). *Children of Glasnost. Growing up Soviet.* Seattle: University of Washington Press.

Pedro, J. (2006). Taking reflection into the real world of teaching. *Kappa Delta Pi Record, 42*(3), 129–132.

Peiser, W. (2000). Cohort replacement and the downward trend in newspaper reading. *Newspaper Research Journal, 21*, 11–23.

Perlman, J., & Waldinger, R. (1997). Second generation decline? Immigrant children past and present: A reconsideration. *International Migration Review, 31*, 893–922.

Perry, T., & Fraser, J. W. (Eds.). (1993). *Freedom's plow: Teaching in the multicultural classroom.* New York: Routledge.

Phelan, P., Davidson, A. L., & Yu, H. C. (1993). Students' multiple worlds: Navigating the borders of family, peer, and school cultures. In P. Phelan & A. L. Davison (Eds.), *Renegotiating cultural diversity in American schools* (pp. 52–88). New York: Teachers College Press.

Phelan, P., Davidson, A. L., & Yu, H. C. (1998). *Adolescents' Worlds.* New York: Teachers College Press.

Portes, A. (1995). Segmented assimilation among new immigrant youth: A conceptual framework. In R. G. Rumbaut & W. A. Cornelius (Eds.), *California's immigrant children: Theory, research and implications for educational policy* (pp. 71–76). San Diego: Center for U.S. Mexican Studies, University of California.

Portes, A., & Rumbaut, R. (2001). *Legacies: The story of immigrant second generation.* Berkeley and New York: University of California Press and Russell Sage Foundation.

Portes, A., & Rumbaut, R. G. (2006). *Immigrant America: A portrait* (3rd ed.) Berkeley and Los Angeles, CA: University of California Press.

Reis-Jorge, J. M. (2005). Developing teachers' knowledge and skills as researchers: A conceptual framework. *Asia Pacific Journal for Teacher Eduxcation, 33*(3), 303–319.

Remennick, L. (2002). Transnational community in the making: Russian-Jewish immigrants of the 1990s in Israel. *Journal of Ethnic and Migration Studies, 28*, 515–530.

Remennick, L. (2007). *Russian Jews on three continents: Identity, integration and conflict.* New Brunswick, NJ: Transaction.

Ribak, R. (1997). Socialization as and through conversation: Political discourse in Israeli families. *Comparative Education Review, 41*(7), 71–96.

Riordan, C. (1990). *Girls and boys in school: Together or separate.* New York: Teachers College Press.

Romaine, S. (1999). *Communicating gender*. London: Erlbaum.

Rosenbloom, S. R., & Way, N. (2004). Experiences of discrimination among African American, Asian American, and Latino adolescents in an urban high school. *Youth & Society, 35*(4), 420–451.

Rosenthal, C. S., Rosenthal, J. A., & Jones, J. (2001). *Social Science Quarterly, 82*(3), 633–646.

Rosiek, J., & Atkinson, B. (2005). Bridging the divides: The need for a pragmatic semiotics of teacher knowledge research. *Educational Theory, 55*(4), 421–442.

Ross, E. W. (2004). Negotiating the politics of citizenship education. *Political Science and Politics, 37*(2), 249–251.

Rumbaut, R. G. (1991). Passages to America: Perspectives on the new immigration. World War II. In A. Wolfe (Ed.), *America at century's end* (pp. 208–244). Berkeley: University of California Press.

Rumbaut, R. G. (1995). The new Californians: Comparative research findings on the educational progress of immigrant children. In R. G. Rumbaut & W. A. Cornelius (Eds.), *California's immigrant children: Theory, research, and implications for educational policy* (pp. 17–69). San Diego, CA: La Jolla, Center for U.S.-Mexican Studies, University of California.

Rumbaut, R. G. (2004). Ages, life stages and generational cohorts: Decomposing the immigrant first and second generation in the United States. *International Migration Review, 38*(3), 1160–1205.

Rumbaut, R. G., & Portes, A., (Eds.). (2001). *Ethnicities: Coming of age in immigrant America*. Totowa, NJ: Rowman & Littlefield.

Rumbaut, R. G., & Portes, A. (Eds.). (2001). Introduction. In *Ethnicities: Children of immigrants in America* (pp. 1–6). Berkeley and New York: University of California Press and Russell Sage Foundation.

Samoff, J. (1991). Socialist education. *Comparative Education Review, 35*(1), 1–22.

Sassen, S. (1996). *Losing control? Sovereignty in the age of globalization*. New York: Columbia University Press.

Schön. D. A. (1987). *Educating the reflective practitioner: Toward a new design of teaching and learning in the professions*. San Francisco: Jossey-Bass.

Segal, D. R., & Kestenbaum, M. (2002). Professional closure in the military labor market: A critique of pure cohesion: In D. M. Snider, G. L. Watkins, & L. J. Matthews (Eds.), *The future of the army profession* (pp. 441–458). Boston: McGraw-Hill.

Shamai, S., & Paul-Binyamin, I. (2004). A model of intensity of multicultural relations: The case of teacher training colleges in Israel. *Race, Ethnicity and Education, 7*, 421–436.

Shaw, T. A. (1994). The semiotic mediation of identity. *Ethos, 22*(1), 83–119.

Sherrod, L. (2004). Promoting the development of citizenship in diverse youth. *Political Science and Politics, 36*(2), 287–292.

Shield, O. (1973). On the meaning of military service in Israel. In M. Curtis & M.S. Chertoff (Eds.), *Israel: Social structure and change* (pp. 419–433). New Brunswick, NJ: Transaction Books.

Shimahara, N. K. (1998). The Japanese model of professional development: Teaching as craft. *Teaching and Teacher Education, 14*, 451–462.

Shumer, R., & Belbas, B. (1996). What we know about service learning. *Education and Urban Society, 28*, 208–223.

Shuval, J. (1998). Migration to Israel: The mythology of "uniqueness." *International Migration, 36*(1), 1–23.

Sigel, R. (1995). New directions for political socialization research: Thoughts and suggestions. *Perspectives on Political Science, 24*(7), 17–22.

Sikron, M., & Leshem, E. (1998). *The portrait of an immigration wave.* Jerusalem: The Hebrew University. Magnes Press (Hebrew).

Sleeter, C. E. (1992). Restructuring schools for multicultural education. *Journal of Teacher Education, 43*, 141–148.

Sloan, K. (2007). High-stakes accountability, minority youth and ethnography: Assessing the multiple effect. *Anthropology and Education Quarterly, 38*(1), 24–41.

Smooha, S. (1978). *Israel: Pluralism and conflict.* Berkeley: University of California Press.

Sorensen, C. (1994), Success and education in South Korea. *Comparative Education Review, 38*(1), 10–35.

Spindler, G., & Spindler, L. (1993). The processes of culture and person: Cultural therapy and culturally diverse schools. In P. Phelan & A. L. Davidson (Eds.), *Renegotiating cultural diversity in American schools* (pp. 27–51). New York: Teachers College Press.

Spindler, G., & Spindler, L. (Eds.). (1994). *Pathways to cultural awareness: Cultural therapy with teachers and students.* Newbury Park, CA: Corwin.

Spiro, M. E. (1966). Buddhism and economic action in Burma, *American Anthropologist, 88*, 1163–1173.

Spradley, J. P. (1979). *The ethnographic interview.* New York: Holt, Rinehart & Winston.

Spradley. J. P. (1980). *Participant observation.* New York: Holt, Rinehart & Winston.

State of Israel Auditor. (1999). *The security system: Absorption of immigrant soldiers in the Israeli Defense Forces.* (From the 50th Report of the State Auditor). Jerusalem: Israeli Government Publications (Hebrew).

Stepick, A., & Stepick, C. D. (2002). Becoming American, constructing ethnicity: Immigrant youth and civic engagement. *Applied Developmental Science, 6*(4), 246–257.

Suárez-Orozco, C. (2004). Formulating identity in a globalized world. In M. Suárez-Orozco & D. B. Qin-Hilliard (Eds.), *Globalization: Culture and education in the new millennium* (pp. 173–202). Berkeley: University of California Press.

Suárez-Orozco, C., & Suárez-Orozco, M. (2001). *Children of immigration.* Cambridge, MA: Harvard University Press.

Suárez-Orozco, C., & Todorova, I. L. G. (2003). The social worlds of immigrant youth. Understanding the social world of immigrant youths. *New Directions for Youth Development, 100* (Winter) (Special issue).

Suárez-Orozco, M. (1989). *Central American refugees and U.S. high schools: A psychological study of motivation and achievement.* Stanford, CA: Stanford University Press.

Suárez-Orozco, M. (Ed.). (2007). *Learning in a global era: International perspectives on globalization and education*. Berkeley: University of California Press.

Suárez-Orozco, M., & Qin-Hilliard, D.B. (Eds.) (2004). *Globalization: Culture and education in the new millennium*. Berkeley: University of California Press.

Suárez-Orozco, M., & Suárez-Orozco, C. (1995). The cultural patterning of achievement motivation: A comparison of Mexican, Mexican immigrant, Mexican American and Non-Latino white American students. In R. G. Rumbaut & W. A. Cornelius (Eds.), *California's immigrant children: Theory, research and implications for educational policy*. San Diego: Center for U.S. Mexican Studies, University of California.

Sunderland, J., & Litosseliti, L. (2002). Gender identity and discourse analysis: Theoretical and empirical considerations. In L. Litosseliti & J. Sunderland (Eds.), *Gender identity and discourse analysis* (pp. 3–42). Amsterdam: John Benjamins.

Swan, J. (2002). Yes, but is it gender. In L. Litosseliti & J. Sunderland (Eds.), *Gender identity and discourse analysis* (pp. 43–68). Amsterdam: John Benjamins.

Swanson, C. B. (2005). Organizational coupling, control and change: The role of higher-order models of control in educational reform. In L. V. Hedges & B. Schneider (Eds.), *The social organization of schooling* (pp. 244–269). New York: Russell Sage.

Tatar, M., & Horenczyk, G. (2003). Diversity related burnout among teachers. *Teaching and Teacher Education*, *19*, 397–408.

Taylor, S. I., & Bogdan, A. (1984). *Introduction to qualitative research methods* (2nd ed.) New York: Wiley.

Taylor, S. V., & Sobel, D. M. (2001). Addressing the discontinuity of students' and teachers' diversity: A preliminary study of preservice teachers' beliefs and perceived skills. *Teaching and Teacher Education*, *17*, 487–503.

Tedin, K. (1980). Assessing peer and parent influence on adolescent political attitudes. *American Journal of Political Science*, *24*(1), 136–154.

Tomiak, J. (Ed.). (1986). *Western perspectives on Soviet education in the 1980s*. New York: St. Martin's.

Toren, N. (2003). Tradition and transition: Family change in Israel. *Gender Issues*, *21*(2), 60–76.

Torney-Purta, J. (2000). Comparative perspectives on political socialization and civic education. *Comparative Education Review*, *44*(7), 88–95.

Torney-Purta, J. (2002). The school's role in developing civic engagement: A study of adolescents in twenty-eight countries. *Applied Developmental Science*, *6*(4), 203–212.

Torney-Purta, J. (2004). Adolescents' political socialization in changing contexts: An International study in the spirit of Nevitt Sanford. *Political Psychology*, *25*(3), 465–478.

Turner, V. (1970). Betwixt and between: The liminal period in rites of passage: In E.A. Hammel & W.A. Simons (Eds.), *Man makes sense* (pp. 364–369). Boston: Little Brown.

Valverde, S. A. (1987). A comparative study of Hispanic high school dropouts and graduates: Why do some leave school early and some finish? *Education and Urban Society*, *19*(3), 320–329.

Van Deth, J., Maraffi, J., Newton, K., & Whiteley, P. F. (1999). *Social capital and European democracy.* London: Routledge.

Van Zanten, A. (1997). Schooling immigrants in France in the 1990s: Success or failure of the republican model of integration. *Anthropology and Education Quarterly, 28*(3), 351–374.

Vertovec, S. (Ed.), (2001). Transnationalism and identity. *Journal of Ethnic and Migration Studies, 27*(4, Special Issue), 573–582.

Waldinger, R., & Feliciano, C. (2004). Will the new second generation experience "downward assimilation?": Segmented assimilation reassessed. *Ethnic and Racial Studies, 27*, 376–402.

Weissbrod, L. (2002). *Israeli identity: In search of the successor to the pioneer, tsabar and settler.* London and Portland, OR: Frank Cass.

Westheimer, J., & Kahne, J. (2004). Educating the "good" citizen: Political choices and pedagogical goals. *Political Science and Politics, 37*(2), 241–247.

Wilkinson, H. (1996). But will they vote? The political attitudes of young people. *Children and Society, 10*(3), 242–244.

Wolcott, H. F. (1975). Criteria for an ethnographic approach to research in schools. *Human Organization, 34*(2), 111–127.

Wolcott, H. F. (1995). *The art of fieldwork.* Thousand Oaks, CA: SAGE.

Wolcott, H. F. (1999). *Ethnography: A way of seeing.* Thousand Oaks, CA: Altamira Press.

Xie, Y., & Goyette, K. A. (2004). *A demographic portrait of Asian Americans. The American people, census 2000.* New York: Russell Sage Foundation of Washington DC, Population Reference Bureau.

Yates, M., & Youniss, J. (Eds.). (1999). *Roots of civic identity: International perspectives on community service and activism in youth.* Cambridge: Cambridge University Press.

Yogev, A. (1996). Practice without policy: Pluralist teacher education in Israel. In M. Craft (Ed.), *Teacher education in plural societies: An international review* (pp. 57–71). Bristol, PA: Palmer Press.

Yogev, A., & Shapira, R. (1990). Citizenship socialization in national voluntary youth organizations. In O. Ichilov (Ed.), *Political socialization, citizenship education and democracy* (pp. 205–219). New York: Teachers College Press.

Zhou, M. (1997). Growing up American: The challenge confronting immigrant children and children of immigrants. *Annual Review of Sociology, 23*, 63–95.

Zhou, M. (2003). Urban education: Challenges in educating culturally diverse children. *Teachers College Record, 105*, 208–225.

Zhou, M., & Xiong, Y.S. (2005). The multifaceted American experiences of the children of Asian immigrants: Lessons for segmented assimilation. *Ethnic and Racial Studies, 28*(6), 1119–1152.

Zilberg, N., & Leshem, E. (1996). Russian-language press and immigrant community in Israel. *Revue Européenne des Migrations Internationales (REMI), 12*(2), 173–189.

ABOUT THE AUTHOR

Rivka A. Eisikovits, PhD, is an associate professor of anthropology and education in the Falculty of Education, University of Haifa, Israel. Her book with M. A. Pitman and M. L. Dobbert on Cultural Acquisition: A Holistic Approach to Human Learning was published by Praeger in 1989. Her book on *The Anthropology of Child and Youth Care Work* was published in 1997 by Haworth Press. Her current research interests include the cross-cultural adaptation of immigrant youth and the study of acculturative encounters. Some of her most recent works on these topics appeared in *Anthropology and Education Quarterly, Comparative Education Review, Higher Education, International Migration, Qualitative Studies in Education, Teaching and Teacher Education,* and *Youth & Society.*

INDEX

Printed in the United States
127977LV00005BA/27/P